Higher
English

Leckie×Leckie

© Scottish Qualifications Authority
All rights reserved. Copying prohibited. No part of this publication may be reproduced, stored in a retrieval system, or transmitted in any form or by any means, electronic, mechanical, photocopying, recording or otherwise.

First exam published in 2004.
Published by Leckie & Leckie Ltd, 3rd Floor, 4 Queen Street, Edinburgh EH2 1JE
tel: 0131 220 6831 fax: 0131 225 9987 enquiries@leckieandleckie.co.uk www.leckieandleckie.co.uk

ISBN 978-1-84372-675-3

A CIP Catalogue record for this book is available from the British Library.

Leckie & Leckie is a division of Huveaux plc.

Leckie & Leckie is grateful to the copyright holders, as credited at the back of the book, for permission to use their material.
Every effort has been made to trace the copyright holders and to obtain their permission for the use of copyright material.
Leckie & Leckie will gladly receive information enabling them to rectify any error or omission in subsequent editions.

[BLANK PAGE]

X115/301

NATIONAL
QUALIFICATIONS
2004

FRIDAY, 14 MAY
9.00 AM – 10.30 AM

ENGLISH
HIGHER
Close Reading

Answer all questions.

50 marks are allocated to this paper.

There are TWO passages and questions in this paper.

Read the passages carefully and then answer all the questions which follow. **Use your own words whenever possible and particularly when you are instructed to do so.**

You should read the passages to:

understand what the writers are saying about the ideas in a book by Frank Furedi called *Paranoid Parenting* (**Understanding—U**);

analyse their choices of language, imagery and structures to recognise how they convey their points of view and contribute to the impact of the passage (**Analysis—A**);

evaluate how effectively they have achieved their purpose (**Evaluation—E**).

A code letter (U, A, E) is used alongside each question to give some indication of the skills being assessed. The number of marks attached to each question will give some indication of the length of answer required.

THB X115/301 6/42220

SCOTTISH
QUALIFICATIONS
AUTHORITY

©

PASSAGE1

The first passage is adapted from an article in The Herald *newspaper in February 2002. In it, Melanie Reid strongly supports the ideas in a book called* Paranoid Parenting *by Frank Furedi.*

IS PARANOID PARENTING THE GREATEST DANGER TO OUR KIDS?

If you read a wonderful new book by sociologist Frank Furedi—*Paranoid Parenting*—you will see the story of a teacher who quit the profession after a school trip was cancelled. Some parents
5 were worried the trip would involve their children in a 45-minute journey in a private car. Would the cars be roadworthy? Were the drivers experienced? Were these no-smoking cars?

Here's another story: once upon a time, there was
10 a little boy who got a new pair of wellies, inside which, around the top, his mother inscribed his name in felt pen. This child, asserting the inalienable rights of small boys everywhere, then proceeded to go out and fill his wellies with water.
15 The ink of his name ran, and by the time the bell rang for school that Monday morning the small boy had vivid blue smudges, like vicious bruises, ringing his calves. His teacher, a zealous young woman, ever alert to the omnipresence of evil,
20 took one look at the marks and lifted the phone to the social work department. "Come quickly," she hissed. "This boy is clearly being abused."

When the social workers rushed to examine the boy and quiz his mother, they could find evidence
25 of nothing. Soap and water had washed away the dreadful bruises, and the mother's relationship with her son turned out to be impeccably healthy. The only mistake this unfortunate family had made was to fulfil society's constant, lurking
30 expectation that all children are in danger all the time.

This may be an urban myth. It matters not. A fairy tale's power lies in its ability to express authentic fears—and this one reveals the
35 paranoia that now prevails where bringing up children is concerned.

We live in an age where parental paranoia has reached absurd heights. Collectively we are now convinced that our children's survival is
40 permanently under threat; worse still, we believe that every incident concerning a child, however benign or accidental, is immediately regarded as a case of bad parenting. We live under perpetual suspicion; and in turn we project it on to everyone
45 around us.

Inevitably, this paranoia has fuelled an artful kind of job creation. When something terrible happens—a sledging accident, a fall from a tree, a scare about "dangerous" foods—the sirens sound
50 and the blue lights flash. This is not just the arrival of the ambulance: it is also a metaphor for the extensive child protection industry gearing itself up for another bout of self-importance. Mee-maw, mee-maw. Clear the area, please. This is a job for the expert doom-mongers. 55

I am tired of these prophets of death and injury. I do not need the Royal Society for the Prevention of Accidents to tell me that children should wear helmets while sledging, because I am incensed at the thought of the hundreds of kids whose 60 parents will now ban them from sledging on the five-million-to-one chance that they might hit a tree. I mourn also for the kids who will never know the delight of cycling with the wind in their hair, or climbing up trees, or exploring hidden 65 places. Growing up devoid of freedom, decision-making, and the opportunity to learn from taking their own risks, our children are becoming trapped, neurotic, and as genetically weakened as battery hens. 70

I am fed up listening to scaremongers about the E-coli virus, telling me my child should never visit a farm or come into contact with animals. I am weary of organisations that are dedicated to promulgating the idea that threats and dangers to 75 children lurk everywhere. I am sick of charities who on the one hand attack overprotective parents and at the same time say children should never be left unsupervised in public places.

Everywhere you turn there is an army of 80 professionals—ably abetted by the media—hard at work encouraging parents to fear the worst. Don't let your children out in the sun—not unless they're wearing special UV-resistant T-shirts. Don't buy your children a Wendy house, they 85 might crush their fingers in the hinges. Don't buy a baby walker, your toddlers might brain themselves. Don't buy plastic baby teethers, your baby might suck in harmful chemicals. Don't let them use mobile phones, they'll sizzle 90 their brains. Don't buy a second-hand car seat, it will not protect them. And on and on it goes.

Teachers are giving up teaching, and youth organisations are dying because they can't find adults prepared to run them. Everywhere good, 95 inspirational people are turning their backs on children because they are terrified of the children and their parents turning on them, accusing them of all manner of wrongdoing. They can no longer operate, they say, in a climate of suspicion and fear. 100

I know how they feel. Some years ago I organised an event for my child's primary school—a running and cycling race along popular, well-used Forestry Commission cycle-tracks.

105 For safety, parents were to be paired with their
offspring; we laid on enough insurance and first
aid for a B-list royal wedding. Yet the event was
almost called off the night before when I
received worried calls from parents who had
110 been out to inspect the route. The track was far
too rough, they said. The risk of children
injuring themselves was too great. It was too
dangerous to proceed. As it happened, we did
go ahead and everyone had a wonderful time.
115 Children glowed with achievement and self-

esteem, unaware of the crisis of parental nerve
which overshadowed the whole day.

But so deep are we in the pit of exaggerated,
irrational risk-perception that we have moved
from the awareness that things might go wrong 120
to the assumption that things *will* go wrong. It is
a dangerous spiral. For our children, who in
reality are overwhelmingly safer than they have
ever been in history from death, disease,
accident, or injury, it is more than dangerous. It 125
is utterly catastrophic.

PASSAGE 2

The second passage is from an article in The Guardian *newspaper, in June 2002. In it, Catherine Bennett takes a slightly
less enthusiastic view of Furedi's ideas.*

PROTECTIVE PARENTS, YES. BUT PARANOID?

It seems the childcare pendulum has swung: the
principal threat to children is no longer
neglectful parents, but excessively protective
ones who are always worrying about germs.

5 Frank Furedi, reader in sociology at the
University of Kent, has written a book, *Paranoid
Parenting*, in which he explores the causes and
far-reaching consequences of too much
cosseting. "It is always important to recall that
10 our obsession with our children's safety is likely
to be more damaging to them than any risks that
they are likely to meet with in their daily
encounter with the world," Furedi writes.

So, far from fretting, like paranoid parents,
15 about the risks of physical injury, Furedi seems
almost nostalgic about them: "Playground areas
are now covered with rubber to limit the damage
when a child does fall." Should they, perhaps, be
constructed from something more challenging:
20 shards of broken glass, say, or the traditional grit
which was once so successful at lacerating young
knees, insinuating itself so deeply into the
exposed tissue that it could only be removed by a
pair of bacteria-infested tweezers?

25 Elsewhere, exploring the degree to which
children's lives are now circumscribed by
parental cowardy custards, Furedi mentions the
dramatic reduction in the number of children
walking to school. In Britain, he notes, parents
30 are more likely to drive their children to school
"than in Germany, Scandinavia or America,
where the distance between home and school

may be far greater". Alas for Furedi's campaign,
some figures published this week are likely to
encourage yet more of this protective behaviour 35
and may even help promote parental paranoia. A
report from UNICEF has found that children in
Britain are among the safest in the world: safer,
for instance, than in Germany, and far safer than
those in America. British children are safer, it 40
seems, precisely because so many of them are
now driven to and from school.

People like Furedi seem to hanker for the time
when bright-eyed schoolboys would think
nothing of trudging several hundred miles to 45
school in their threadbare socks, negotiating
such major arterial roads as existed in the olden
days, sustained only by a few strands of linty
liquorice and the prospect of a tepid miniature of
school milk. Such hazards as the young scamps 50
might meet along the way—electrical storms,
say, or runaway trains, or a modest invasion of
Martians—merely added to the character-
building nature of the exercise.

Perhaps parents who would, given a choice, 55
prefer their children to be minimally hurt when
they fall off a climbing frame or into a pond are
not being paranoid—just being careful. Maybe
the real paranoiacs are not those who worry
about their children being squashed by 60
sociopaths in cars, but those who insist on adding
the consequences of mollycoddling to the
already overlong catalogue of parental anxieties.

Questions on Passage 1

		Marks	Code

1. How does the story told in the first paragraph (lines 1–8) help you to understand the meaning of the word "paranoid"? — **2** — **U**

2. Read the story the writer tells in lines 9–31.

   (a) State briefly the main point of this story in conveying the writer's argument. — **1** — **U**

   (b) How does the writer's word choice in these lines make clear her attitude **either** to the teacher **or** to the social workers? — **2** — **A**

3. "It matters not." (line 32)

Explain in your own words why the writer believes it is not important whether this story is true or not. — **2** — **U**

4. Read lines 37–55.

   (a) How does the writer's language in lines 37–45 emphasise her belief that "parental paranoia has reached absurd heights" (lines 37–38)? — **2** — **A**

   (b) (i) What is the writer's attitude to "the expert doom-mongers" (line 55)? — **1** — **U**

      (ii) How does her language in lines 46–55 make this attitude clear? — **2** — **A**

5. "… as genetically weakened as battery hens …" (lines 69–70)

   (a) Why, according to the writer, are modern children in danger of becoming like this? Refer to lines 56–70 and use your own words as far as possible in your answer. — **2** — **U**

   (b) How effective do you find the image of "battery hens" in conveying the writer's view of the way children are currently being brought up? — **2** — **A/E**

6. Read lines 71–92.

   (a) (i) Identify the tone of lines 71–79. — **1** — **A**

      (ii) Explain how this tone is conveyed. — **2** — **A**

   (b) How does the language of lines 80–92 emphasise the writer's feelings about the "army of professionals" (lines 80–81)?

In your answer you should refer to at least **two** techniques such as sentence structure, tone, word choice … — **4** — **A**

7. Why, according to the writer in lines 93–100, are teachers and youth workers "turning their backs on children" (lines 96–97)? Use your own words as far as possible in your answer. — **2** — **U**

8. How effective do you find the personal anecdote in lines 101–117 in supporting the writer's point of view in the passage so far? — **3** — **U/E**

9. By referring to **one** technique, show how the writer demonstrates in the final paragraph (lines 118–126) the intensity of her feelings on the subject. — **2** — **A**

                                                      (30)

Questions on Passage 2

10. Read lines 1–24.

   (a) Explain how the image in the opening paragraph (lines 1–4) supports the writer's point. — **2** — **A**

   (b) How does the context in which it is used help you to understand the meaning of the word "cosseting" (line 9)? — **2** — **U**

   (c) (i) Explain in your own words what Furedi thinks about modern play areas. — **1** — **U**

      (ii) What is the writer's attitude to Furedi's point of view and how is this made clear by the tone of lines 18 ("Should they …")–24? — **2** — **A**

11. "Alas for Furedi's campaign …" (line 33)

Explain in your own words how the UNICEF report contradicts Furedi's point of view. — **2** — **U**

12. Show how the writer's attitude to Furedi's views is conveyed in lines 43–54. — **4** — **A**

13. Explain in your own words the main points the writer makes in her concluding paragraph (lines 55–64). — **2** — **U**

                                                      (15)

Question on both Passages

14. Which writer's response to Furedi's views are you more inclined to agree with?

You must refer closely to the ideas of both passages as evidence for your answer. — **5** — **U/E**

                                                      (5)

[END OF QUESTION PAPER]

                                                   Total (50)

X115/302

NATIONAL
QUALIFICATIONS
2004

FRIDAY, 14 MAY
10.50 AM – 12.20 PM

ENGLISH
HIGHER
Critical Essay

Answer **two** questions.

Each question must be taken from a different section.

Each question is worth 25 marks.

SCOTTISH
QUALIFICATIONS
AUTHORITY

©

Answer TWO questions from this paper.

Each question must be chosen from a different Section (A–E). You are not allowed to choose two questions from the same Section.

In all Sections you may use Scottish texts.

Write the number of each question chosen in the margin of your answer booklet and begin each essay on a fresh page. You should spend about 45 minutes on each essay.

The following will be assessed:

- **the relevance of your essays to the questions you have chosen**

- **the quality of your writing**

- **the technical accuracy of your writing.**

Each answer is worth up to 25 marks. The total for this paper is 50 marks.

SECTION A—DRAMA

1. Choose a play in which your attitude to a central character varies at different stages of the action.

   Show how the skill of the dramatist causes your attitude to change.

   In your answer you must refer closely to the text and to at least **two** of: characterisation, language, key scene(s), setting, or any other appropriate feature.

2. Choose a play in which the dramatist explores the idea of rebellion against authority.

   Explain briefly the circumstances which give rise to the rebellion and discuss how successfully you think the dramatist explores the idea.

   In your answer you must refer closely to the text and to at least **two** of: theme, soliloquy, conflict, characterisation, or any other appropriate feature.

3. Choose a play in which there is a scene involving intense emotion.

   Show how the dramatist makes you aware of the intensity of the emotion in the scene and discuss the importance of the scene to the drama as a whole.

   In your answer you must refer closely to the text and to at least **two** of: conflict, characterisation, soliloquy, dialogue, or any other appropriate feature.

4. Choose a play which you have read and watched in performance.

   Compare your reading of a key scene with its presentation in performance.

   In your answer you must refer closely to the text and to at least **two** of: dialogue, characterisation, casting, stage set, or any other appropriate feature.

SECTION B—PROSE

5. Choose a **novel** in which your admiration for a particular character grows as the plot unfolds.

    Explain briefly why your admiration increases and, in more detail, discuss how the writer achieves this.

    In your answer you must refer closely to the text and to at least **two** of: characterisation, theme, key incidents, structure, or any other appropriate feature.

6. Choose a **novel** or **short story** in which the writer's use of setting in time and/or place has a significant part to play in your appreciation of the text as a whole.

    Give the relevant details of the setting and then discuss fully why it has such significance.

    In your answer you must refer closely to the text and to at least **two** of: setting, narrative stance, theme, characterisation, or any other appropriate feature.

7. Choose a **novel** which had such an impact on you that you still reflect upon its message.

    Explain why the novel has had such an impact on you.

    In your answer you must refer closely to the text and to at least **two** of: theme, key incidents, characterisation, structure, or any other appropriate feature.

8. Choose a **novel** or **short story** which reaches a climax which you find dramatic or moving or disturbing.

    Explain how the writer achieves the effect and discuss how it contributes to your appreciation of the text as a whole.

    In your answer you must refer closely to the text and to at least **two** of: structure, theme, characterisation, dialogue, or any other appropriate feature.

9. Choose a **non-fiction text** in which the writer puts forward an opinion which you found totally convincing.

    Explain what the writer's view is and, in more detail, discuss how this view was presented in a way that convinced you.

    In your answer you must refer closely to the text and to at least **two** of: ideas, evidence, stance, style, or any other appropriate feature.

10. Choose a **non-fiction text** which increased your interest in a particular leisure activity.

    Give a brief description of the activity and explain, in more detail, what it was about the writer's presentation of it that captured your interest.

    In your answer you must refer closely to the text and to at least **two** of: choice of detail, anecdote, language, structure, or any other appropriate feature.

11. Choose a **non-fiction text** in which the writer's ability to evoke a sense of place is very important to the success of the text.

    Show how the writer's presentation of the location(s) enhanced your appreciation of the text.

    In your answer you must refer closely to the text and to at least **two** of: setting, anecdote, stance, mood, or any other appropriate feature.

[Turn over

SECTION C—POETRY

12. Choose a poem in which the poet explores the significance of the passage of time.

    Explain why the passage of time is significant in this poem and discuss the means by which the poet explores its significance.

    In your answer you must refer closely to the text and to at least **two** of: mood, form, theme, imagery, or any other appropriate feature.

13. Choose **two** love poems.

    By comparing the treatment of the subject in each poem, discuss which you find more successful.

    In your answer you must refer closely to the text and to at least **two** of: structure, word choice, imagery, sound, or any other appropriate feature.

14. Choose a poem in which a chance encounter or a seemingly unimportant incident acquires increased significance by the end of the poem.

    Show how the poet's development of the encounter or incident leads you to a deeper understanding of the poem's theme.

    In your answer you must refer closely to the text and to at least **two** of: theme, atmosphere, word choice, rhythm, or any other appropriate feature.

15. Choose a poem in which the poet creates a picture of a heroic or a corrupt figure.

    Discuss the means by which the personality is clearly depicted.

    In your answer you must refer closely to the text and to at least **two** of: imagery, tone, rhyme, word choice, or any other appropriate feature.

SECTION D—MASS MEDIA

16. Choose a film which belongs to a specific genre such as horror, fantasy, film noir, western.

    How well did the film exploit or develop the features of the genre in dealing with its subject matter?

    In your answer you must refer closely to the text and to at least **two** of: mise-en-scène, soundtrack, editing, casting, or any other appropriate feature.

17. Choose a *TV drama in which conflict between or within groups, factions or families provides a major interest.

    Describe the nature of the conflict and show how this conflict is presented to sustain your interest in the drama.

    In your answer you must refer closely to the text and to at least **two** of: structure, characterisation, setting, use of camera, or any other appropriate feature.

18. Choose a film which casts light on an issue of political, social or moral concern.

    Identify the issue and show how the film makers illuminated it for you.

    In your answer you must refer closely to the text and to at least **two** of: theme, mise-en-scène, editing, plot, or any other appropriate feature.

19. Choose an important character from a film or *TV drama whose presentation in your opinion has outstanding visual impact.

    Briefly outline the importance of this character in the film or drama and go on to show how the character is developed primarily through images.

    In your answer you must refer closely to the text and to at least **two** of: mise-en-scène, characterisation, editing, casting, or any other appropriate feature.

*"TV drama" can be a single play, a series or a serial.

SECTION E—LANGUAGE

20. Consider the language of persuasion as used in the political or commercial world.

    By referring to one such persuasive use of language, discuss how successful you feel it was in fulfilling its purpose.

    You must refer to specific examples and to at least **two** of the following: word choice, tone, presentation, structure, or any other appropriate feature.

21. Consider the spoken language of a particular locality.

    Identify some of the characteristics of the language of this locality and discuss to what extent it fulfils a valuable function within the community.

    You must refer to specific examples and to at least **two** of the following: dialect, accent, vocabulary, register, or any other appropriate feature.

22. Consider the language of newspaper reporting (broadsheet and/or tabloid) associated with such subjects as war, sport, crime, environmental disasters.

    Identify some of the characteristics of this language and discuss how effective you feel it was in conveying the events described.

    You must refer to specific examples and to at least **two** of the following: word choice, illustration, presentation, point of view, or any other appropriate feature.

23. Consider the language associated with a particular group in society which shares a common interest or background.

    Identify the aspects of language which are special to this group and discuss to what extent these aspects facilitate communication within the group.

    You must refer to specific examples and to at least **two** of the following: word choice, register, abbreviation, jargon, or any other appropriate feature.

[END OF QUESTION PAPER]

[BLANK PAGE]

[BLANK PAGE]

X115/301

NATIONAL
QUALIFICATIONS
2005

FRIDAY, 13 MAY
9.00 AM – 10.30 AM

ENGLISH
HIGHER
Close Reading

Answer all questions.

50 marks are allocated to this paper.

There are TWO passages and questions.

Read the passages carefully and then answer all the questions which follow. **Use your own words whenever possible and particularly when you are instructed to do so.**

You should read the passages to:

understand what the writers are saying about the threat to earth from comets and asteroids (**Understanding—U**);

analyse their choices of language, imagery and structures to recognise how they convey their points of view and contribute to the impact of the passage (**Analysis—A**);

evaluate how effectively they have achieved their purpose (**Evaluation—E**).

A code letter (U, A, E) is used alongside each question to give some indication of the skills being assessed. The number of marks attached to each question will give some indication of the length of answer required.

SCOTTISH
QUALIFICATIONS
AUTHORITY

©

PASSAGE 1

The first passage is the Introduction to a book called "IMPACT! The Threat of Comets and Asteroids" by Gerrit L Verschuur, a well-known scientist. He explores past impacts caused by comets and asteroids and goes on to look at the probability of further collisions. He raises questions about the future of the human race and asks what, in light of the knowledge we have, we should do now.

THE THREAT OF COMETS AND ASTEROIDS

The discovery that a comet impact triggered the disappearance of the dinosaurs as well as more than half the species that lived 65 million years ago may have been the most significant scientific
5 breakthrough of the twentieth century. Brilliant detective work on the part of hundreds of scientists in analysing clues extracted from the study of fossils, and by counting the objects in near-earth space, has allowed the dinosaur
10 mass-extinction mystery to be solved. As a result we have gained new insight into the nature of life on earth.

A lot has been learned about the nature of cosmic collisions and this new knowledge has given a
15 remarkable twist to the story of our origins. We now recognise that comet and asteroid impacts may be the most important driving force behind evolutionary change on the planet. Originally, such objects smashed into one another to build
20 the earth 4·5 million years ago. After that, further comet impacts brought the water of our oceans and the organic molecules needed for life. Ever since then, impacts have continued to punctuate the story of evolution. On many occasions,
25 comets slammed into earth with such violence that they nearly precipitated the extinction of all life. In the aftermath of each catastrophe, new species emerged to take the place of those that had been wiped out.

30 We have now recognised the fundamental role of comet and asteroid collisions in shaping evolutionary change and this recognition means that the notion of "survival of the fittest" may have to be reconsidered. Survivors of essentially
35 random impact catastrophes—cosmic accidents —were those creatures who just happened to be "lucky" enough to find themselves alive after the dust settled. It doesn't matter how well a creature may have been able to survive in a particular
40 environment *before* the event—being thumped on the head by a large object from space *during* the event is not conducive to a long and happy existence.

Our new understanding of why the dinosaurs
45 and so many of their contemporary species became extinct has revealed the earth as a planet not specifically designed for our well-being. From time to time, life is rudely interrupted by shattering events on a scale we can barely
50 imagine.

For more than two centuries the possibility that the earth might be struck by comets has been debated and three questions have been raised from the start: will a comet again hit the earth;
55 might comet impact lead to the extinction of mankind; is it possible that the flood legends from so many world cultures could be explained by past comet impact in the oceans which triggered enormous tsunamis? In recent years
60 most scientists have come to accept that the answer to the first two questions is probably yes.

The third of these questions has begun again to excite interest, but here the implications of an affirmative answer reach beyond the scientific.
65 Great prejudice exists both for and against the idea that the legendary "Flood" was a real event triggered by asteroid or comet impact. To accept this possibility challenges the long-held beliefs of many people who see the event as having religious
70 significance. However, recent breakthroughs in our understanding of cosmic collisions have cast new light on what might lie behind ancient beliefs, legends, sagas and myths that tell of terrible floods that once ravaged the world.

75 In comparison with more immediate threats to the continued survival of our species (acid rain, destruction of stratospheric ozone, the greenhouse effect, overpopulation), the danger of comet or asteroid impacts may seem remote.
80 The problem with impact events, however, is that their consequences are so awesome that we can barely imagine what it would be like to be struck by a large object from space. And there would be limited opportunity for reflection following such
85 an event.

There is also an irony attached to the acquisition of our knowledge of the threat of comets and asteroids. We know that cosmic collisions clearly set the scene for the emergence of *Homo sapiens*,
90 our species. We have recently become conscious enough to design and manipulate instruments such as radio-telescopes which allow us to explore beyond our senses. In so doing, we have come to behold how our species fits into the
95 cosmic scheme of things and to foresee the dangers.

Once we appreciate that impact catastrophes have shaped life as we know it, and that such events will happen again in the future, how will
100 this awareness alter the way we see ourselves in the cosmic context? Will we let nature take its course and trust to luck that our species will

survive the next violent collision? Or will we confront the forces that may yet influence the 105 destiny of all life on earth?

Many details referred to in our story are still controversial. Debate is particularly heated as regards the role of impacts in directing the course of human history. All of this is very 110 exciting. The whole topic is in a state of ferment, a symptom that something significant is brewing.

Ultimately we must ask ourselves whether we find the risk of future impact to be sufficiently great to merit doing something to avoid it. 115 Many dangers posed by living in a modern technological society are far more likely to cost us our lives, but that is not the point. Rare comet or asteroid impacts may cost *all* of us our lives. So how will the threat of comets and asteroids fit 120 into our thinking? We can only answer this question after we have learned a great deal more about the nature of the danger.

PASSAGE 2

The second passage is adapted from an article in a national tabloid newspaper.

ASTEROID COULD BLAST US BACK TO DARK AGES

It would destroy an area the size of Belgium in one and a half seconds and plunge the world back into the Dark Ages. The giant lump of space rock racing towards Earth today at 75,000 5 miles an hour would unleash a force 20 million times more powerful than the atom bomb dropped on Hiroshima in 1945. If it ends up crashing into us on 21st March 2014, that is.

Asteroid QQ47, two thirds of a mile wide, was 10 first spotted by astronomers in Mexico ten days ago and is hurtling towards us at twenty miles a second. A direct hit by the huge asteroid would send billions of tons of dust into the sky, blocking out the sun, causing plant life to perish 15 and livestock to starve. The effect on human life, too, would be devastating. But perhaps we needn't worry too much—because scientists say the chances of it hitting us are just 1 in 909,000.

Astrophysics expert, Dr Alan Fitzsimmons of 20 Queen's University, Belfast, who advises the UK NEO (Near-Earth Objects) Information Centre in Leicester, is optimistic that Earth will come through the latest asteroid scare unscathed: "In all probability, within the next 25 month we will know its future orbit with an accuracy which will mean we will be able to rule out any impact."

Others are, however, convinced that it is only a matter of time before we face Armageddon. 30 Liberal Democrat MP and sky-watcher, Lembit Opik, says: "I have said for years that the chance of an asteroid having an impact which could wipe out most of the human race is 100 per cent." He has raised his worries in the 35 Commons, successfully campaigning for an all-party task force to assess the potential risk and helped set up the Spaceguard UK facility to track near-earth objects. He admits: "It does

sound like a science fiction story and I may sound like one of those guys who walk up and 40 down with a sandwich-board saying the end of the world is nigh. But the end *is* nigh."

Asteroids have long been a source of fascination for scientists and range in size from tiny dust particles to huge objects nearly 600 miles across. 45 More than 100,000 asteroids have been classified since the first was spotted by Italian astronomer Guiseppe Piazzi in 1801. Some contain carbon-bearing compounds and scientists think they could hold the key to 50 creation. Giant meteors hitting the planet could have delivered chemicals which kick-started life on Earth.

But now asteroid QQ47 could end man's fragile reign. Spaceguard director, Jay Tate, explains: 55 "In the longer term the problem of being hit by an asteroid will be the amount of material that is injected into the Earth's atmosphere. Within two or three days the surface of the Earth will be cold and dark. And it is the dark which will be 60 the problem, because the plants will begin to die out. At best guess, we will probably lose about 25 per cent of the human population of the planet in the first six months or so. The rest of us are basically back in the Middle Ages. We have 65 got no power, no communications, no infrastructure. We are back to hunter-gathering."

Although there are hundreds of undiscovered asteroids hurtling around, bookmakers are 70 willing to take bets at odds of 909,000 to 1 that QQ47 will snuff out mankind. After all, as one bookmaker says happily: "If the asteroid does wipe out life on Earth, we probably won't have to worry about paying out to winning 75 customers."

Questions on Passage 1

		Marks	*Code*

1. (*a*) According to the first sentence of the passage, what important discovery has been made about comet impact? Use your own words as far as possible in your answer. **2** **U**

(*b*) By referring to lines 5–12 ("Brilliant . . . on earth."), describe briefly **one** method scientists used to find the evidence for this discovery. **1** **U**

2. (*a*) Explain, using your own words as far as possible, what is meant by "the most important driving force behind evolutionary change on the planet" (lines 17–18). **2** **U**

(*b*) Using your own words as far as possible, give any two examples from lines 18–29 which the writer uses to illustrate the point being made in lines 17–18. **2** **U**

(*c*) How does the language of lines 18–29 highlight the writer's ideas? You should refer to at least two of the following techniques: structure, word choice, imagery. **4** **A**

3. Read lines 30–43.

(*a*) Explain in your own words why the writer thinks that the theory of the "survival of the fittest" will have to be reconsidered. **2** **U**

(*b*) Explain how the writer creates a slightly humorous tone in lines 34–43. **2** **A**

4. What does "Our new understanding" (line 44) about the extinction of other species lead us to think about our own relationship with the planet? Use your own words as far as possible in your answer. **1** **U**

5. How does the writer's use of punctuation in lines 51–59 ("For more . . . tsunamis?") help you to understand what he is saying? **2** **A**

6. Referring to lines 62–74, explain in your own words one way in which the "third of these questions" leads into an area which may be described as "beyond the scientific" (line 64). **2** **U**

7. In lines 75–85, the writer deals with various threats to the survival of our species.

Show how effective the last sentence "And there would be . . . event." (lines 83–85) is as a conclusion to this paragraph. **2** **E**

8. Explain briefly in your own words what, according to the writer, is "an irony" about "our knowledge of the threat of comets and asteroids". You should refer to lines 86–96 in your answer. **2** **U**

9. (*a*) According to the writer in lines 97–105, what two possible courses of action are open to us with regard to future "impact catastrophes"? Use your own words as far as possible in your answer. **2** **U**

(*b*) Show how effective you find the writer's use of imagery in lines 106–112 in conveying the excitement of the "debate". **2** **A/E**

(*c*) Which course of action do you think the writer favours? Support your answer by close reference to lines 113–123. **2** **U**

(30)

Questions on Passage 2

10. Show how the writer captures your attention in the opening to the article (lines 1–18). You should refer to specific techniques and/or stylistic features in these lines. **4** **A**

11. By commenting on specific words or phrases in lines 19–27, show to what extent you would have confidence in Dr Alan Fitzsimmons. **2** **A/E**

12. Show how lines 28–42 help you to understand the meaning of the word "Armageddon" (line 29). **2** **U**

13. The style of writing in lines 43–53 differs from that in the preceding paragraphs.

Describe these two different styles and support your answer by brief reference to the text. **2** **A**

14. Show how Jay Tate's language (lines 56–68) emphasises the devastating effects of asteroid impact. In your answer you should refer to such features as sentence structure, verb tense, word choice . . . **4** **A**

15. Explain why the bookmaker is speaking "happily" (line 73). **1** **U**

(15)

Question on both Passages

16. Which passage do you find more effective in making you think about the implications for the human race of comet and asteroid impact? Justify your choice by referring to the **ideas and style** of **both passages**. **5** **E**

(5)

Total (50)

[*END OF QUESTION PAPER*]

X115/302

NATIONAL
QUALIFICATIONS
2005

FRIDAY, 13 MAY
10.50 AM – 12.20 PM

ENGLISH
HIGHER
Critical Essay

Answer **two** questions.

Each question must be taken from a different section.

Each question is worth 25 marks.

SCOTTISH
QUALIFICATIONS
AUTHORITY

Answer TWO questions from this paper.

Each question must be chosen from a different Section (A–E). You are not allowed to choose two questions from the same Section.

In all Sections you may use Scottish texts.

Write the number of each question chosen in the margin of your answer booklet and begin each essay on a fresh page. You should spend about 45 minutes on each essay.

The following will be assessed:

- **the relevance of your essays to the questions you have chosen**

- **the quality of your writing**

- **the technical accuracy of your writing.**

Each answer is worth up to 25 marks. The total for this paper is 50 marks.

SECTION A—DRAMA

1. Choose a play in which a character is seeking the truth, avoiding the truth or hiding the truth.

    Explain to what extent the character achieves this aim and discuss how the dramatist uses the situation to reveal important aspects of the character's role in the play as a whole.

    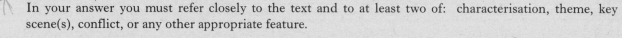

    In your answer you must refer closely to the text and to at least two of: characterisation, theme, key scene(s), conflict, or any other appropriate feature.

2. Choose a play which features **one** of the following themes: appearance versus reality; good versus evil; dreams versus reality; youth versus age.

    Show how the dramatist develops one of these themes and discuss how the exploration of this theme enhances your appreciation of the play as a whole.

    In your answer you must refer closely to the text and to at least two of: conflict, characterisation, key scene(s), structure, or any other appropriate feature.

3. Choose a play in which the dramatist creates a sense of mystery at or near the beginning of the play.

    Show how the dramatist creates the sense of mystery and then discuss to what extent the resolution of the mystery is important to the play as a whole.

    In your answer you must refer closely to the text and to at least two of: key scene(s), theme, setting, atmosphere, or any other appropriate feature.

4. Choose a play in which the mood is mainly dark or pessimistic.

    Show how the dramatist creates this mood and discuss how appropriate it is to the main idea(s) of the play.

    In your answer you must refer closely to the text and to at least two of: setting, theme, characterisation, dialogue, or any other appropriate feature.

SECTION B—PROSE

Prose Fiction

5. Choose a **novel** in which an incident reveals a flaw in a central character.

   Explain how the incident reveals this flaw and go on to discuss the importance of the flaw in your understanding of the character.

   In your answer you must refer closely to the text and to at least two of: key incident(s), theme, characterisation, structure, or any other appropriate feature.

6. Choose a **novel** or **short story** in which the writer's method of narration (such as first person narrative, diary form, journal . . .) plays a significant part.

   Explain briefly the method of narration and then discuss its importance to your appreciation of the text.

   In your answer you must refer closely to the text and to at least two of: narrative technique, tone, characterisation, structure, or any other appropriate feature.

7. Choose a **novel** in which the story's emotional twists ensure that your interest is held until the end.

   Briefly explain how these twists involve you in the story and then discuss how they lead to a deeper appreciation of the text as a whole.

   In your answer you must refer closely to the text and to at least two of: characterisation, structure, theme, key incident(s), or any other appropriate feature.

8. Choose a **novel** or **short story** in which the fate of a main character is important in conveying the writer's theme.

   Explain what you consider the theme to be and discuss how effectively the fate of the character conveys it.

   In your answer you must refer closely to the text and to at least two of: theme, plot, characterisation, setting, or any other appropriate feature.

Prose Non-fiction

9. Choose an example of **biography** or **autobiography** which gave you a detailed insight into a person's life.

   Explain how the writer's presentation made you think deeply about the person and his or her life.

   In your answer you must refer closely to the text and to at least two of: style, anecdotes, setting, ideas, or any other appropriate feature.

10. Choose a **non-fiction text** in which the writer's presentation of an experience triggers an emotional response from you.

    Give a brief description of the experience and, in more detail, explain how the writer's presentation has this effect.

    In your answer you must refer closely to the text and to at least two of: choice of detail, language, stance, structure, or any other appropriate feature.

11. Choose a **non-fiction text** in which the writer puts forward views on a social issue.

    Explain the writer's stance on the issue and then discuss in detail to what extent the writer's presentation influenced your point of view.

    In your answer you must refer closely to the text and to at least two of: language, evidence, stance, setting, or any other appropriate feature.

[Turn over

SECTION C—POETRY

12. Choose a poem in which a specific setting is strongly evoked.

    Show how the poet creates this sense of place and/or time, and then discuss the relative importance of the setting to the poem as a whole.

    In your answer you must refer closely to the text and to at least two of: setting, theme, mood, imagery, or any other appropriate feature.

13. Choose a poem which you feel is particularly relevant to a teenage audience.

    Make clear why you think the poem is so relevant to this age group and show how the poetic techniques used in the poem help to achieve this.

    In your answer you must refer closely to the text and to at least two of: theme, mood, imagery, rhythm, or any other appropriate feature.

14. Choose a poem in which humour (for example, satire, wit or irony) plays a significant part.

    Show how the poet makes the poem humorous and discuss how important the humour is to the underlying message of the poem.

    In your answer you must refer closely to the text and to at least two of: ideas, tone, rhyme, word choice, or any other appropriate feature.

15. Choose a poet whose writing displays great beauty.

    By referring to one **or** more than one poem, show how the writer creates this sense of beauty and go on to discuss whether or not the beauty of the writing is more important to you than the ideas explored in the poem(s).

    In your answer you must refer closely to the text(s) and to at least two of: imagery, sound, rhythm, word choice, theme, or any other appropriate feature.

SECTION D—MASS MEDIA

16. Choose a film or *TV drama in which an individual or group is threatened by an evil force.

    Briefly explain the situation and go on to show how successfully the film/programme makers use this situation to provoke audience response.

    You must refer to specific examples and to at least two of the following: characterisation, mise-en-scène, editing, soundtrack, or any other appropriate feature.

17. Choose a film or *TV drama in which a particular mood is constructed through key images and elements of the soundtrack.

    Show how the film or programme makers construct this mood and go on to explain how it influences your appreciation of the text as a whole.

    You must refer to specific examples and to at least two of the following: mood, soundtrack, mise-en-scène, editing, or any other appropriate feature.

18. Choose a film where the makers challenge certain conventions of a particular genre such as Western, Horror, Science Fiction, Film Noir.

    Show how the film makers challenge these conventions and go on to explain how this approach affects your appreciation of the genre.

    You must refer to specific examples and to at least two of the following: genre, theme, characterisation, plot, or any other appropriate feature.

19. Choose a film or *TV drama in which the past plays a crucial role.

    Show how the film or programme makers reveal the significance of the past and why it is important to your appreciation of key elements of the text.

    You must refer to specific examples and to at least two of the following: editing, mise-en-scène, plot, character, or any other appropriate feature.

*"TV drama" includes a single play, a series or a serial.

SECTION E—LANGUAGE

20. Consider the spoken language of a particular generation—young children, teenagers, an older generation, for example.

    Identify what you consider to be the particular aspects of language which typify this group, and show to what extent these aspects of language operate to the benefit of the generation to which they belong.

    You must refer to specific examples and to at least two of the following language concepts: vocabulary, grammar, dialect, accent, or any other appropriate concept.

21. Consider the language used to communicate with the general public in specialist areas such as legal, financial, medical, or government services.

    Identify the areas of difficulty in such communications and show to what extent the provider of any of these services has succeeded in overcoming these difficulties.

    You must refer to specific examples and to at least two of the following language concepts: vocabulary, register, jargon, sentence structure, or any other appropriate concept.

22. Consider any form of Scots, either written or spoken, with which you are familiar.

    To what extent are the users of your chosen form of Scots advantaged or disadvantaged?

    You must refer to specific examples and to at least two of the following language concepts: vocabulary, grammar, accent, tone, or any other appropriate concept.

23. Consider the contribution made to English by the language of other parts of the world during the last 100 years or so—for example, the languages of the Indian Sub-Continent, the USA, Continental Europe, the Caribbean . . .

    By identifying contributions made to English, discuss to what extent it gains from its ability to "borrow" words, phrases and idioms from other languages.

    You must refer to specific examples and to at least two of the following language concepts: vocabulary, slang, idiom, grammar, or any other appropriate concept.

[END OF QUESTION PAPER]

[BLANK PAGE]

[BLANK PAGE]

X115/301

NATIONAL
QUALIFICATIONS
2006

FRIDAY, 12 MAY
9.00 AM – 10.30 AM

ENGLISH
HIGHER
Close Reading—Text

There are TWO passages and questions.

Read the passages carefully and then answer all the questions, which are printed in a separate booklet.

You should read the passages to:

understand what the writers are saying about problems of diet and obesity in the modern world (**Understanding—U**);

analyse their choices of language, imagery and structures to recognise how they convey their points of view and contribute to the impact of the passage (**Analysis—A**);

evaluate how effectively they have achieved their purpose (**Evaluation—E**).

SCOTTISH
QUALIFICATIONS
AUTHORITY

PASSAGE 1

The first passage is from an article in The Economist *magazine in December 2003. In it, the writer explores the problem of obesity in the modern world.*

THE SHAPE OF THINGS TO COME

When the world was a simpler place, the rich were fat, the poor were thin, and right-thinking people worried about how to feed the hungry. Now, in much of
5 the world, the rich are thin, the poor are fat, and right-thinking people are worrying about obesity.

Evolution is mostly to blame. It has designed mankind to cope with
10 deprivation, not plenty. People are perfectly tuned to store energy in good years to see them through lean ones. But when bad times never come, they are stuck with that energy, stored around
15 their expanding bellies.

Thanks to rising agricultural productivity, lean years are rarer all over the globe. Pessimistic economists, who used to draw graphs proving that the
20 world was shortly going to run out of food, have gone rather quiet lately. According to the UN, the number of people short of food fell from 920m in 1980 to 799m 20 years later, even though
25 the world's population increased by 1·6 billion over the period. This is mostly a cause for celebration. Mankind has won what was, for most of his time on this planet, his biggest battle: to ensure that
30 he and his offspring had enough to eat. But every silver lining has a cloud, and the consequence of prosperity is a new plague that brings with it a host of interesting policy dilemmas.

35 There is no doubt that obesity is the world's biggest public-health issue today—the main cause of heart disease, which kills more people these days than

AIDS, malaria, war; the principal risk factor in diabetes; heavily implicated in 40 cancer and other diseases. Since the World Health Organisation labelled obesity an epidemic in 2000, reports on its fearful consequences have come thick and fast. 45

Will public-health warnings, combined with media pressure, persuade people to get thinner, just as such warnings finally put them off tobacco? Possibly. In the rich world, sales of healthier foods are 50 booming and new figures suggest that over the past year Americans got very slightly thinner for the first time in recorded history. But even if Americans are losing a few ounces, it will be many 55 years before their country solves the health problems caused by half a century's dining to excess. And everywhere else in the economically developed world, people are still piling 60 on the pounds.

That's why there is now a worldwide consensus among doctors that governments should do something to stop them. There's nothing radical about 65 the idea that governments should intervene in the food business. They've been at it since 1202, when King John of England first banned the adulteration of bread. Governments and the public 70 seem to agree that ensuring the safety and stability of the food supply is part of the state's job. But obesity is a more complicated issue than food safety. It is not about ensuring that people don't get 75 poisoned: it is about changing their behaviour.

Should governments be trying to do anything about it at all?

80 There is one bad reason for doing something, and two good reasons. The bad reason is that governments should help citizens look after themselves. People, the argument goes, are misled by

85 their genes, which are constantly trying to pack away a few more calories just in case of a famine around the corner. Governments should help guide them towards better eating habits. But that

90 argument is weaker in the case of food than it is for tobacco—nicotine is addictive, chocolate is not—and no better than it is in any other area where people have a choice of being sensible or

95 silly. People are constantly torn by the battle between their better and worse selves. It's up to them, not governments, to decide who should win.

A better argument for intervention is
100 that dietary habits are established early in childhood. Once people get fat, it is hard for them to get thin; once they are used to breakfasting on chips and fizzy drinks, that's hard to change. The state, which

105 has some responsibility for moulding minors, should try to ensure that its small citizens aren't mainlining sugar at primary school. Britain's government is gesturing towards tough restrictions on

110 advertising junk food to children. That seems unlikely to have much effect. Sweden already bans advertising to children, and its young people are as porky as those in comparable countries. Other moves, such as banning junk food 115 from schools, might work better. In some countries, such as America, soft-drinks companies bribe schools to let them install vending machines. That should stop. 120

A second plausible argument for intervention is that thin people subsidise fat people through contributions to the National Health Service. If everybody is forced to carry the weight of the seriously 125 fat, then everybody has an interest in seeing them slim down. That is why some people believe the government should tax fattening food—sweets, snacks and take-aways. They argue this 130 might discourage consumption of unhealthy food and recoup some of the costs of obesity.

It might; but it would also constitute too great an intrusion on liberty for the gain 135 in equity and efficiency it might (or might not) represent. Society has a legitimate interest in fat, because fat and thin people both pay for it. But it also has a legitimate interest in not having the 140 government stick its nose too far into the private sphere. If people want to eat their way to grossness and an early grave, let them.

[Turn over

PASSAGE 2

The second passage appeared as an article in The Observer *newspaper in May 2004. In it, Susie Orbach, a clinician who has worked for many years with people suffering from eating problems, suggests that there are different views on the "obesity epidemic".*

FOOLISH PANIC IS ABOUT PROFIT

At primary school, my son's lunch-box was inspected and found to fail. It contained chocolate biscuits. The school, believing it was doing the right
5 thing, had banned sweets, chocolates and crisps in the name of good nutrition.

After school and in the playground, away from the teachers' eyes, sweets and chocolates were traded. They became
10 the marks of rebellion and the statements of independence. Eating foods they suspected the grown-ups would rather they didn't, made those foods ever so much more enticing. They
15 weren't just food but food plus attitude.

The school was well-meaning—just misguided. Its attitude, like most of what permeates the obesity debate, has turned good intentions into
20 bad conclusions. Despite endless thoughtful discussion on the subject, we are left with a sense that obesity is about to destabilise the NHS, that dangerous fat is swamping the nation.

25 That there is a considerable increase in obesity is not in question. The extent of it is. For many, obesity is a source of anguish and severe health difficulties. But the motivation of some of those who
30 trumpet these dangers associated with obesity needs to be questioned. There is considerable evidence that there is serious money to be made from a condition in search of treatment, and
35 the categorisation of fat may just fit this bill perfectly. In the US, commercial slimming clubs and similar groups contributed millions of dollars to Shape Up America, an organisation which was
40 part of a strategy to turn obesity into a disease which can be treated by the pharmaceutical, diet and medical industries. Medicine is, after all, an industry in the US.

45 So sections of the market aim to profit from the notion that we are all too fat. We need to contest that. It isn't the case. Evidence from the professional journals shows that fitness, not fat,
50 determines our mortality. You can be fat, fit and healthy.

We are in danger of being too willing to mimic the US dogma on the demonisation of fat and of particular
55 foods. This matters because it creates a climate in which the government may fail to ask fundamental questions about whose interests are served by the introduction of hysteria around obesity;
60 particularly who profits and who hurts. A corrective to the scare tactics is needed. People should consider, for example, the simple fact that the new rise in obesity is not simple growth, but
65 is partly due to the body mass index (BMI) being revised downwards in the past six years. If you are Brad Pitt, you are now considered overweight. If you are as substantial as Russell Crowe, you
70 are obese. Overnight 36 million Americans woke up to find that they were obese.

The hidden psychological effects of this attack on our body size are enormous.
75 We are not going to protect the next generation by simply exhorting them to eat so-called good foods.

There is a lot to be done. We need to address what food means in people's emotional lives. We need to transform
80 the culture of thinness. We need to recognise that we as a society are deeply confused about eating and dieting. And we need to realise that part of this confusion has been cynically promoted
85 by those who now are selling us the obesity epidemic.

[END OF TEXT]

X115/302

NATIONAL QUALIFICATIONS 2006	FRIDAY, 12 MAY 9.00 AM – 10.30 AM	**ENGLISH** HIGHER Close Reading–Questions

Answer all questions. **Use your own words whenever possible and particularly when you are instructed to do so.**

50 marks are allocated to this paper.

A code letter (U, A, E) is used alongside each question to give some indication of the skills being assessed. The number of marks attached to each question will give some indication of the length of answer required.

SCOTTISH
QUALIFICATIONS
AUTHORITY

Questions on Passage 1   *Marks* *Code*

1. Read the first paragraph (lines 1–7).

   (*a*) Explain briefly how the concerns of "right-thinking people" have changed
   over time.   1   U

   (*b*) Identify **two** ways by which the sentence structure in these lines emphasises
   the change.   2   A

2. "Evolution is mostly to blame." (line 8)

   How does the writer go on to explain this statement? You should refer to lines 8–15
   and use your own words as far as possible.   2   U

3. Read lines 16–34.

   (*a*) Why, according to lines 16–26, have the "pessimistic economists . . . gone
   rather quiet"?   1   U

   (*b*) "This is mostly a cause for celebration." (lines 26–27)

   What evidence does the writer provide in lines 27–34 to support this
   statement?   2   U

   (*c*) How effective do you find the imagery of lines 27–34 in illustrating the
   writer's line of thought? You must refer to **two** examples in your answer.   4   A/E

4. How does the writer's language in lines 35–45 stress the seriousness of the health
   problem?

   In your answer you should refer to at least two features such as sentence structure,
   word choice, tone . . .   4   A

5. Identify from lines 46–61 one cause for hope and one cause for concern. Use your
   own words as far as possible.   2   U

6. In lines 62–133 the writer moves on to discuss the arguments for and against
   government intervention in the food industry.

   (*a*) According to lines 62–77, what was the purpose of government intervention
   in the past, and what is a further purpose of its intervention now?   2   U

   (*b*) Read carefully lines 80–133.

   Summarise the key points of the "one bad reason" and the "two good reasons"
   (lines 80–81) for government intervention in food policy. You must use your
   own words as far as possible.   6   U

7. In the final paragraph (lines 134–144) the writer makes clear that he disapproves of
   too much government intervention.

   Show how the writer uses particular features of language to demonstrate his
   strength of feeling.   4   A

                                                                        (30)

	Marks	Code
Questions on Passage 2		

8. "The school was well-meaning—just misguided." (lines 16–17)

    (a) How do lines 1–15 demonstrate this?   **2**   **U**

    (b) Show how the writer's word choice in lines 7–15 makes clear the children's attitude to the school's ban.   **2**   **A**

9. Read lines 25–44.

    Identify what, according to the writer, is the "motivation" referred to in line 29, and show in your own words how it is illustrated in lines 36–44.   **3**   **U**

10. Show how the sentence structure in lines 45–51 highlights the writer's views about the obesity debate.   **2**   **A**

11. "A corrective to the scare tactics is needed." (lines 61–62)

    (a) Show how the language of lines 52–60 supports the connotation(s) of the expression "scare tactics".   **2**   **A**

    (b) Explain in your own words how lines 62–72 suggest a "corrective" to the scare tactics.   **2**   **U**

12. How does the writer's language in the final paragraph (lines 78–87) highlight her belief that action is required on this issue?   **2**   **A**

    (15)

Questions on both Passages

13. Consider lines 1–45 of Passage 1 and lines 1–51 of Passage 2.

    In these lines each writer presents the opening stages of an argument about obesity.

    (a) Briefly state an important difference between the two **points of view** as set out in these lines.   **1**   **U**

    (b) By comparing the **style** of these lines, show which you find more effective in capturing your interest.   **4**   **A/E**

    (5)

    Total (50)

[END OF QUESTION PAPER]

[BLANK PAGE]

X115/303

NATIONAL QUALIFICATIONS 2006	FRIDAY, 12 MAY 10.50 AM – 12.20 PM	**ENGLISH HIGHER** Critical Essay

Answer **two** questions.

Each question must be taken from a different section.

Each question is worth 25 marks.

SCOTTISH QUALIFICATIONS AUTHORITY

©

Answer TWO questions from this paper. Each question must be chosen from a different Section (A–E). You are not allowed to choose two questions from the same Section.

In all Sections you may use Scottish texts.

Write the number of each question in the margin of your answer booklet.

You should spend about 45 minutes on each essay.

The following will be assessed:

- the relevance of your essays to the questions you have chosen, and the extent to which you sustain an appropriate line of thought

- your knowledge and understanding of key elements, central concerns and significant details of the chosen texts, supported by detailed and relevant evidence

- your understanding, as appropriate to the questions chosen, of how relevant aspects of structure/style/language contribute to the meaning/effect/impact of the chosen texts, supported by detailed and relevant evidence

- your evaluation, as appropriate to the questions chosen, of the effectiveness of the chosen texts, supported by detailed and relevant evidence

- the quality of your written expression and the technical accuracy of your writing.

SECTION A—DRAMA

Answers to questions on drama should address relevantly the central concern(s)/theme(s) of the text and be supported by reference to appropriate dramatic techniques such as: conflict, characterisation, key scene(s), dialogue, climax, exposition, dénouement, structure, plot, setting, aspects of staging (such as lighting, music, stage set, stage directions . . .), soliloquy, monologue . . .

1. Choose a play in which the dramatist's use of contrast between two characters is important to your understanding of one of them.

   Discuss how your understanding of this character is strengthened by the contrast.

2. Choose a play in which the conclusion leaves you with mixed emotions but clearly conveys the dramatist's message.

   Briefly explain how the mixed emotions are aroused by the conclusion and then discuss how you are given a clear understanding of the message of the play as a whole.

3. Choose a play which underlines how one person's flaw(s) can have a significant impact on other people as well as on himself or herself.

   Explain briefly the nature of the flaw(s) and then, in detail, assess how much the character and others are affected.

4. Choose a play in which an important theme is effectively highlighted by one specific scene or incident.

   Explain how the theme is explored in the play as a whole and then show in detail how the chosen scene or incident effectively highlights it.

SECTION B—PROSE

Prose Fiction

Answers to questions on prose fiction should address relevantly the central concern(s)/theme(s) of the text(s) and be supported by reference to appropriate techniques of prose fiction such as: characterisation, setting, key incident(s), narrative technique, symbolism, structure, climax, plot, atmosphere, dialogue, imagery . . .

5. Choose a **novel** or **short story** in which a central character's failure to understand the reality of his or her situation is an important feature of the text.

   Explain how the writer makes you aware of this failure and show how it is important to your appreciation of the text as a whole.

6. Choose a **novel**, set in a time different from your own, with a theme relevant to the world today.

   Show how you are led to an appreciation of the theme's continuing relevance, despite its setting in time.

7. Choose a **novel** or **short story** which you feel has a particularly well-chosen title.

   Explain why you think the title helps you to appreciate the central idea(s) of the text.

8. Choose a **novel** in which a key incident involves rejection or disappointment or loss.

   Describe briefly the key incident and assess its significance to the text as a whole.

Prose Non-fiction

Answers to questions on prose non-fiction should address relevantly the central concern(s)/theme(s) of the text and be supported by reference to appropriate techniques of prose non-fiction such as: ideas, use of evidence, selection of detail, point of view, stance, setting, anecdote, narrative voice, style, language, structure, organisation of material . . .

9. Choose an **essay** or **piece of journalism** which has made an impact on you because of its effective style.

   Discuss how the writer's style adds to the impact of the content.

10. Choose a **non-fiction text** which provides insight into a country or a personality or a lifestyle.

    Describe briefly the country or personality or lifestyle and discuss the means by which the writer leads you to this insight.

11. Choose a **non-fiction text** which explores a significant aspect of political or cultural life.

    Show how the writer's presentation enhances your understanding of the chosen aspect of political or cultural life.

[Turn over

SECTION C—POETRY

Answers to questions on poetry should address relevantly the central concern(s)/theme(s) of the text(s) and be supported by reference to appropriate poetic techniques such as: imagery, verse form, structure, mood, tone, sound, rhythm, rhyme, characterisation, contrast, setting, symbolism, word choice . . .

12. Choose a poem in which there is a noticeable change of mood at one or more than one point in the poem.

    Show how the poet conveys the change(s) of mood and discuss the importance of the change(s) to the central idea of the poem.

13. Choose a poem which deals with a childhood experience.

    Discuss to what extent the poet's description of the experience leads you to a clear understanding of the poem's theme.

14. Choose **two** poems by the same poet which you consider similar in theme and style.

    By referring to theme and style in both poems, discuss which poem you prefer.

15. Choose a poem which explores one of the following subjects: bravery, compassion, tenderness.

    Show how the poet's exploration of the subject appeals to you emotionally and/or intellectually.

SECTION D—FILM AND TV DRAMA

> *Answers to questions on film and TV drama should address relevantly the central concern(s)/theme(s) of the text(s) and be supported by reference to appropriate techniques of film and TV drama such as: key sequence(s), characterisation, conflict, structure, plot, dialogue, editing/montage, sound/soundtrack, aspects of mise-en-scène (such as lighting, colour, use of camera, costume, props . . .), mood, setting, casting, exploitation of genre . . .*

16. Choose a **film** or ***TV drama** the success of which is built on a central figure carefully constructed to appeal to a particular audience.

    Show how the film or programme makers construct this figure and explain why he/she/it appeals to that particular audience.

17. Choose a **film** or ***TV drama** in which a power struggle shapes the lives of key characters and/or groups.

    Discuss how effectively the film or programme makers establish the power struggle and go on to explain how it shapes the lives of the key characters and/or groups.

18. Choose a **film** in which the film makers have presented an epic story to critical and/or box office acclaim.

    Show how the film makers convey key epic elements and explain why you think the film has received such acclaim.

19. Choose a **film** or ***TV drama** which is based on a novel and successfully captures such elements of the book as setting, character, mood and theme.

    Show how the film or programme makers successfully capture any two elements of the novel.

*"TV drama" includes a single play, a series or a serial.

[Turn over

SECTION E—LANGUAGE

Answers to questions on language should address relevantly the central concern(s) of the language research/study and be supported by reference to appropriate language concepts such as: register, jargon, tone, vocabulary, word choice, technical terminology, presentation, illustration, accent, grammar, idiom, slang, dialect, structure, vocabulary, point of view, orthography, abbreviation . . .

20. Consider the use of language to influence public opinion.

    Identify some of the ways in which language is used to influence the public's view on an issue of public interest. Evaluate the success of at least two of these ways.

21. Consider some of the differences between spoken language used in informal contexts and spoken language used in formal contexts.

    Identify some of the areas of difference and show to what extent the different forms are effective for the contexts in which they are used.

22. Consider the language—spoken or written—which is typically used by a group of people with a common leisure or vocational interest.

    To what extent is the specialist language effective in:

    • describing the details and procedures connected with the group's common interest and/or

    • reinforcing the interaction within the group?

23. Consider any one electronic means of communication introduced over the last forty years or so.

    To what extent has your chosen means of communication developed its own form of language? By examining aspects of this language discuss what you feel are its advantages and/or disadvantages.

[END OF QUESTION PAPER]

[BLANK PAGE]

X115/301

NATIONAL
QUALIFICATIONS
2007

FRIDAY, 11 MAY
9.00 AM – 10.30 AM

ENGLISH
HIGHER
Close Reading—Text

There are TWO passages and questions.

Read the passages carefully and then answer all the questions, which are printed in a separate booklet.

You should read the passages to:

understand what the writers are saying about the proposal to put online the contents of some major libraries (**Understanding—U**);

analyse their choices of language, imagery and structures to recognise how they convey their points of view and contribute to the impact of the passage (**Analysis—A**);

evaluate how effectively they have achieved their purpose (**Evaluation—E**).

SCOTTISH
QUALIFICATIONS
AUTHORITY
©

PASSAGE 1

In the first passage George Kerevan, writing in The Scotsman *newspaper in December 2003, responds to the prospect of an "online library".*

DESPITE GOOGLE, WE STILL NEED GOOD LIBRARIES

The internet search engine Google, with whom I spend more time than with my loved ones, is planning to put the contents of the world's greatest university libraries online, including the Bodleian in Oxford and those of Harvard and Stanford in America. Part of me is ecstatic at the thought of all that information at my
5 fingertips; another part of me is nostalgic, because I think physical libraries, book-lined and cathedral-quiet, are a cherished part of civilisation we lose at our cultural peril.

My love affair with libraries started early, in the Drumchapel housing scheme in the Fifties. For the 60,000 exiles packed off from slum housing to the city's outer
10 fringe, Glasgow Council neglected the shops and amenities but somehow remembered to put in a public library—actually, a wooden shed. That library was split into two—an adult section and a children's section. This was an early taste of forbidden fruit. Much useful human reproductive knowledge was gained from certain books examined surreptitiously in the adult biology section.

15 At university, I discovered the wonder of the library as a physical space. Glasgow University has a skyscraper library, built around a vast atrium stretching up through the various floors. Each floor was devoted to a different subject classification. Working away on the economics floor, I could see other students above or below—chatting, flirting, doodling, panicking—all cocooned in their own separate
20 worlds of knowledge. Intrigued, I soon took to exploring what was on these other planets: science, architecture, even a whole floor of novels. The unique aspect of a physical library is that you can discover knowledge by accident. There are things you know you don't know, but there are also things you never imagined you did not know.

25 There is a stock response to my love affair with libraries: that I am being too nostalgic. That the multi-tasking, MTV generation can access information from a computer, get cheap books from the supermarket and still chatter to each other at a thousand decibels. Who needs old-fashioned library buildings? And why should councils subsidise what Google will provide for free?

30 There is some proof for this line of argument. The number of people in Scotland using their local public library falls every year, with just under a quarter of Scots now borrowing books (admittedly, that was 34 million books). As a result, local authorities have reduced their funding for new books by 30 per cent. Of course, fewer new books mean fewer library users, so guaranteeing the downward spiral.

35 It may well be that public demand and technical change mean we no longer need the dense neighbourhood network of local libraries of yore. But our culture, local and universal, does demand strategically situated libraries where one can find the material that is too expensive for the ordinary person to buy, or too complex to find online. Such facilities are worth funding publicly because the return in informed
40 citizenship and civic pride is far in excess of the money spent.

Libraries also have that undervalued resource—the trained librarian. The ultimate Achilles' heel of the internet is that it presents every page of information as being

equally valid, which is of course nonsense. The internet is cluttered with false information, or just plain junk. The library, with its collection honed and developed
45 by experts, is a guarantee of the quality and veracity of the information contained therein, something that Google can never provide.

Libraries have another function still, which the internet cannot fulfil. Libraries, like museums, are custodians of knowledge—and should be funded as such. It has become the fashion in recent decades to turn our great national libraries and
50 museums into entertainment centres, with audio-visuals, interactive displays and gimmicks. While I have some enthusiasm for popularising esoteric knowledge, it cannot always be reduced to the level of a child's view of the universe. We have a duty to future generations to invest in the custodians of our culture, in particular its literature and manuscripts.

55 Of course, I can't wait for Google to get online with the Bodleian Library's one million books. Yet here's one other thing I learned from a physical library space: the daunting scale of human knowledge and our inability to truly comprehend even a fraction of it. On arriving at Glasgow University library, I did a quick calculation of how many economics books there were on the shelves and realised that I could
60 not read them all. Ever. From which realisation comes the beginning of wisdom—and that is very different from merely imbibing information.

PASSAGE 2

In the second passage Ben Macintyre, writing in The Times *newspaper, also in December 2003, responds to the same news, and considers the future of the "traditional library".*

PARADISE IS PAPER, PARCHMENT AND DUST

I have a halcyon library memory. I am sitting under a cherry tree in the tiny central courtyard of the Cambridge University Library, a book in one hand and an almond slice in the other. On the grass beside me is an incredibly pretty girl. We are surrounded by eight million books. Behind the walls on every side of the
5 courtyard, the books stretch away in compact ranks hundreds of yards deep, the shelves extending at the rate of two miles a year. There are books beneath us in the subterranean stacks, and they reach into the sky; we are entombed in words, an unimaginable volume of collected knowledge in cold storage, quiet and vast and waiting.

10 Perhaps that was the moment I fell in love with libraries.

Or perhaps it was earlier, growing up in Scotland, when the mobile library would lurch up the road with stocks of Enid Blyton for the kids and supplies of bodice-rippers on the top shelf with saucy covers, to be giggled over when the driver-librarian was having his cup of tea.

15 Or perhaps the moment came earlier yet, when my father took me deep into the Bodleian in Oxford and I inhaled, for the first time, that intoxicating mixture of paper, parchment and dust.

I have spent a substantial portion of my life since in libraries, and I still enter them with a mixture of excitement and awe. I am not alone in this. Veneration for
20 libraries is as old as writing itself, for a library is more to our culture than a

collection of books: it is a temple, a symbol of power, the hushed core of civilisation, the citadel of memory, with its own mystique, social and sensual as well as intellectual.

But now a revolution, widely compared to the invention of printing itself, is taking
25 place among the book shelves, and the library will never be the same again. This week Google announced plans to digitise fifteen million books from five great libraries, including the Bodleian.

Some fear that this total library, vast and invisible, could finally destroy traditional libraries, which will become mere warehouses for the physical objects, empty of
30 people and life. However, the advantages of a single scholarly online catalogue are incalculable and rather than destroying libraries, the internet will protect the written word as never before, and render knowledge genuinely democratic. Fanatics always attack the libraries first, dictators seek to control the literature, elites hoard the knowledge that is power. Shi Huangdi, the Chinese emperor of the 3rd century BC,
35 ordered that all literature, history and philosophy written before the founding of his dynasty should be destroyed. More books were burnt in the 20th century than any other—in Nazi Germany, Bosnia and Afghanistan. With the online library, the books will finally be safe, and the bibliophobes will have been beaten, for ever.

But will we bother to browse the shelves when we can merely summon up any book
40 in the world with the push of a button? Are the days of the library as a social organism over? Almost certainly not, for reasons psychological and, ultimately, spiritual. Locating a book online is one thing, reading it is quite another, for there is no aesthetic substitute for the physical object; the computer revolution rolls on inexorably, but the world is reading more paper books than ever.

45 And the traditional library will also survive, because a library is central to our understanding of what it is to be human. Libraries are not just for reading in, but for sociable thinking, exploring and exchanging ideas. They were never silent. Technology will not change that, for even in the starchiest heyday of Victorian self-improvement, libraries were intended to be meeting places of the mind, recreational
50 as well as educational. The Openshaw branch of the Manchester public library was built complete with a billiard room. Of course just as bookshops have become trendy, offering brain food and cappuccinos, so libraries, under financial and cultural pressure, will have to evolve by more actively welcoming people in to wander and explore . . . and fall in love.

55 Bookish types have always feared change and technology, but the book, and the library, have adapted and endured, retaining their essential magic. Even Hollywood understood. In the 1957 film *Desk Set*, Katherine Hepburn plays a librarian-researcher whose job is threatened by a computer expert (Spencer Tracy) introducing new technology. In the end, the computer turns out to be an asset, not a
60 danger, Tracy and Hepburn end up smooching, and everyone reads happily ever after.

The marriage of Google and the Bodleian will surely be the same.

[*END OF TEXT*]

X115/302

NATIONAL QUALIFICATIONS 2007	FRIDAY, 11 MAY 9.00 AM – 10.30 AM	ENGLISH HIGHER Close Reading–Questions

Answer all questions. **Use your own words whenever possible and particularly when you are instructed to do so.**

50 marks are allocated to this paper.

A code letter (U, A, E) is used alongside each question to give some indication of the skills being assessed. The number of marks attached to each question will give some indication of the length of answer required.

SCOTTISH
QUALIFICATIONS
AUTHORITY

Questions on Passage 1   *Marks   Code*

1. Read lines 1–7.

   (*a*) What two contrasting emotions does the writer have about the plan to put the great university libraries online? Use your own words in your answer.   2   U

   (*b*) How does the writer's word choice in these lines help to convey his view of the importance of "physical libraries" (line 5)? Refer to **two** examples in your answer.   2   A

2. In your opinion, does the writer think Glasgow Council gave the library in Drumchapel a high priority? Justify your answer by close reference to lines 8–14.   2   U/E

3. Show how the writer uses imagery **and** word choice in lines 15–24 to convey the "wonder of the library as a physical space".   4   A

4. Read lines 25–34.

   (*a*) Show how the writer's language in lines 25–29 conveys his attitude to the "MTV generation". You should refer in your answer to such features as sentence structure, word choice, tone . . .   3   A

   (*b*) Explain the "downward spiral" (line 34) to which the writer refers.   1   U

5. (*a*) In your own words as far as possible, give **four** reasons the writer presents in lines 35–46 in favour of maintaining traditional public libraries.   4   U

   (*b*) Show how the writer's word choice in lines 41–46 emphasises the contrast between his attitude to libraries and his attitude to the internet.   2   A

6. Read lines 47–54.

   (*a*) Twice in this paragraph the writer refers to libraries as "custodians". What does this word mean?   1   U

   (*b*) Show how the language of lines 47–54 suggests that the writer has some reservations about the entertainment aspect of present day libraries and museums.   2   A

7. How effective do you find the ideas and/or language of the final paragraph (lines 55–61) as a conclusion to the passage as a whole?   3   E

                                                              (26)

		Marks	Code
Questions on Passage 2			

8. Read lines 1–17.

   (*a*) Briefly describe the mood created in lines 1–3 ("I have . . . girl."). — **1** — **U**

   (*b*) Show how the writer's use of language in lines 3–9 ("We are . . . waiting.") conveys a sense of awe. — **3** — **A**

   (*c*) How effective do you find the repetition of "perhaps" (lines 10–17) in conveying the writer's recollections about libraries? — **2** — **A/E**

9. By referring to **one** example, show how the writer's imagery in lines 18–23 conveys the importance of libraries. — **2** — **A**

10. Read lines 24–38.

    In your own words as far as possible, explain:

    (*a*) what, according to the writer, the potential disadvantage of the online library is; — **1** — **U**

    (*b*) what, according to the writer, the advantages of the online library are. — **3** — **U**

11. Read lines 39–54.

    (*a*) Explain what the writer means by "there is no aesthetic substitute for the physical object" (lines 42–43). — **2** — **U**

    (*b*) Using your own words as far as possible, explain why the writer believes libraries will "survive" (line 45). — **2** — **U**

12. How effectively does the writer use the reference to the film *Desk Set* to conclude the passage in a pleasing way? Refer in your answer to the ideas and language of lines 55–62. — **3** — **E**

(19)

Question on both Passages

13. Which of the two writers do you think presents the more persuasive argument in favour of public libraries?

    Justify your choice by referring to the **ideas and style** of **both** passages. — **5** — **E**

(5)

Total (50)

[END OF QUESTION PAPER]

[BLANK PAGE]

X115/303

NATIONAL
QUALIFICATIONS
2007

FRIDAY, 11 MAY
10.50 AM – 12.20 PM

ENGLISH
HIGHER
Critical Essay

Answer **two** questions.

Each question must be taken from a different section.

Each question is worth 25 marks.

PB X115/303 6/43870

SCOTTISH
QUALIFICATIONS
AUTHORITY

Answer TWO questions from this paper. Each question must be chosen from a different Section (A–E). You are not allowed to choose two questions from the same Section.

In all Sections you may use Scottish texts.

Write the number of each question in the margin of your answer booklet and begin each essay on a fresh page.

You should spend about 45 minutes on each essay.

The following will be assessed:

- the relevance of your essays to the questions you have chosen, and the extent to which you sustain an appropriate line of thought

- your knowledge and understanding of key elements, central concerns and significant details of the chosen texts, supported by detailed and relevant evidence

- your understanding, as appropriate to the questions chosen, of how relevant aspects of structure/style/language contribute to the meaning/effect/impact of the chosen texts, supported by detailed and relevant evidence

- your evaluation, as appropriate to the questions chosen, of the effectiveness of the chosen texts, supported by detailed and relevant evidence

- the quality of your written expression and the technical accuracy of your writing.

SECTION A—DRAMA

Answers to questions on drama should address relevantly the central concern(s)/theme(s) of the text and be supported by reference to appropriate dramatic techniques such as: conflict, characterisation, key scene(s), dialogue, climax, exposition, dénouement, structure, plot, setting, aspects of staging (such as lighting, music, stage set, stage directions . . .), soliloquy, monologue . . .

1. Choose a play which has a theme of revenge or betrayal or sacrifice.

    Show how the dramatist explores your chosen theme and discuss how this treatment enhances your appreciation of the play as a whole.

2. Choose from a play an important scene which you found particularly entertaining or particularly shocking.

    Explain briefly why the scene is important to the play as a whole and discuss in detail how the dramatist makes the scene so entertaining or shocking.

3. Choose a play in which a character makes a crucial error.

    Explain what the error is and discuss to what extent it is important to your understanding of the character's situation in the play as a whole.

4. Choose a play in which the relationship between a male and a female character changes significantly.

    Show how the relationship between the two characters changes and discuss to what extent this illuminates a central idea of the play.

SECTION B—PROSE

Prose Fiction

Answers to questions on prose fiction should address relevantly the central concern(s)/theme(s) of the text(s) and be supported by reference to appropriate techniques of prose fiction such as: characterisation, setting, key incident(s), narrative technique, symbolism, structure, climax, plot, atmosphere, dialogue, imagery . . .

5. Choose a **novel** in which a character reaches a crisis point.

   Explain briefly how this point is reached and go on to discuss how the character's response to the situation extends your understanding of him/her.

6. Choose **two short stories** in which aspects of style contribute significantly to the exploration of theme.

   Compare the ways in which stylistic features are used to create and maintain your interest in the central ideas of the texts.

7. Choose a **novel** with an ending which you found unexpected.

   Explain briefly in what way the ending is unexpected and go on to discuss to what extent it is a satisfactory conclusion to the novel.

8. Choose a **novel** or **short story** in which one of the main characters is not in harmony with her/his society.

   Describe the character's situation and go on to discuss how it adds to your understanding of a central concern of the text.

Prose Non-fiction

Answers to questions on prose non-fiction should address relevantly the central concern(s)/theme(s) of the text and be supported by reference to appropriate techniques of prose non-fiction such as: ideas, use of evidence, selection of detail, point of view, stance, setting, anecdote, narrative voice, style, language, structure, organisation of material . . .

9. Choose a work of **non-fiction** which deals with **travel** or **exploration** or **discovery**.

   Discuss to what extent the presentation of the text reveals as much about the writer's personality and/or views as it does about the subject matter.

10. Choose a **biography** or **autobiography** in which the life of the subject is presented in an effective and engaging way.

    Show how the writer uses techniques of non-fiction to achieve this.

11. Choose an **essay** or **piece of journalism** which appeals to you because it is both informative and passionate.

    Explain what you learned about the topic and discuss how the writer's presentation conveys his/her passion.

[Turn over

SECTION C—POETRY

> *Answers to questions on poetry should address relevantly the central concern(s)/theme(s) of the text(s) and be supported by reference to appropriate poetic techniques such as: imagery, verse form, structure, mood, tone, sound, rhythm, rhyme, characterisation, contrast, setting, symbolism, word choice . . .*

12. Choose a poem in which there is a sinister atmosphere or person or place.

    Show how the poet evokes this sinister quality and discuss how it adds to your appreciation of the poem.

13. Choose **two** poems on the same theme which impress you for different reasons.

    Compare the treatment of the theme in the two poems and discuss to what extent you find one more impressive than the other.

14. Choose a poem in which there is effective use of one or more of the following: verse form, rhythm, rhyme, repetition, sound.

    Show how the poet effectively uses the feature(s) to enhance your appreciation of the poem as a whole.

15. Choose a poem involving a journey which is both literal and metaphorical.

    Discuss how effectively the poet describes the journey and makes you aware of its deeper significance.

SECTION D—FILM AND TV DRAMA

Answers to questions on film and TV drama should address relevantly the central concern(s)/theme(s) of the text(s) and be supported by reference to appropriate techniques of film and TV drama such as: key sequence(s), characterisation, conflict, structure, plot, dialogue, editing/montage, sound/soundtrack, aspects of mise-en-scène (such as lighting, colour, use of camera, costume, props . . .), mood, setting, casting, exploitation of genre . . .

16. Choose a **film** or **TV drama*** the success of which is built on a rivalry or friendship between two characters.

    Show how the film or programme makers construct the characters and discuss how the rivalry or friendship contributes to the success of the text.

17. Choose a **film** in which music makes a significant contribution to the impact of the film as a whole.

    Show how the film makers make use of music, and go on to explain how its contribution is so important relative to other elements of the text.

18. Choose a **film** or **TV version** of a stage play or of a novel.

    By referring to key elements of the film or TV version, explain to what extent you think the film or programme makers were successful in transferring the play or novel to the screen.

19. Choose a **film** or **TV drama*** in which setting and atmosphere contribute more than plot to your appreciation of the text.

    Justify your opinion by referring to these elements of the text.

*"TV drama" includes a single play, a series or a serial.

[Turn over

SECTION E—LANGUAGE

Answers to questions on language should address relevantly the central concern(s) of the language research/study and be supported by reference to appropriate language concepts such as: register, jargon, tone, vocabulary, word choice, technical terminology, presentation, illustration, accent, grammar, idiom, slang, dialect, structure, point of view, orthography, abbreviation . . .

20. Consider the spoken or written language of a particular geographical area. (This could be, for example, a village, a city, or a larger area of the UK.)

Identify what is distinctive about the language and evaluate the effects of these distinctive usages on the communication of the people of that area.

21. Consider the language of popular entertainment in the 21st century—in TV, radio, music, magazines, for example.

Describe how the idioms and vocabulary popularised by the entertainment industry influence the everyday speech of the younger generation. Discuss to what extent these usages enrich everyday communication.

22. Consider the language of persuasion employed in a commercial, political, social or personal situation.

Identify and discuss the effectiveness of several ways in which the language you have chosen attempts to be persuasive.

23. Consider the language typical of any particular vocational or interest group with which you are familiar.

To what extent are the specialist terms and idioms typical of this group a barrier to the ability of the general public to understand the communication? How necessary do you think these terms and idioms are for effective communication within the group?

[END OF QUESTION PAPER]

[BLANK PAGE]

X115/301

NATIONAL
QUALIFICATIONS
2008

THURSDAY, 15 MAY
9.00 AM – 10.30 AM

ENGLISH
HIGHER
Close Reading—Text

There are TWO passages and questions.

Read the passages carefully and then answer all the questions, which are printed in a separate booklet.

You should read the passages to:

understand what the writers are saying about the countryside and those who campaign to protect it (**Understanding—U**);

analyse their choices of language, imagery and structures to recognise how they convey their points of view and contribute to the impact of the passage (**Analysis—A**);

evaluate how effectively they have achieved their purpose (**Evaluation—E**).

PASSAGE 1

In this extract from his book "Shades of Green", David Sinclair looks at attitudes to the countryside and discusses to what extent it is part of "our heritage".

RURAL MANIA

The "countryside debate" has rarely been out of the news in Britain in recent years. Reading the newspapers, watching television, listening to the radio, entering a bookshop, one could be forgiven for thinking that we still live in small peasant communities dependent upon the minutest shift in agricultural policy. Sometimes it
5 has seemed almost as if we were still in the early nineteenth century when we relied on the countryside to survive, so extensive have been the debates, so fierce the passions aroused.

One faction has cried constantly that the countryside is in mortal danger from greedy developers whose only motive is profit; another has kept on roaring that
10 farmers are killing every wild thing in sight and threatening the very soil on which we stand through overuse of machinery and chemicals; still another has been continually heard ululating over a decline in the bird population, or the loss of hedgerows, or the disappearance of marshland, or the appearance of coniferous forest.

15 Then there is the proliferation of action groups dedicated to stopping construction of roads, airports, railway lines, factories, shopping centres and houses in rural areas, while multifarious organisations have become accustomed to expending their time and energies in monitoring and reporting on the state of grassland, water, trees, moorlands, uplands, lowlands, birds' eggs, wildflowers, badgers, historical sites and
20 countless other aspects of the landscape and its inhabitants.

It might be thought—indeed, it is widely assumed—that it must be good for the countryside to be returned to the central position it enjoyed in British life long ago. Yet there is a particularly worrying aspect of the new rural mania that suggests it might finally do the countryside more harm than good.

25 This is the identification, in the current clamour, of the countryside in general and the landscape in particular with the past—the insistence on the part of those who claim to have the best intentions of ruralism at heart that their aim is to protect what they glibly refer to as "our heritage". This wildly over-used term is seriously misleading, not least because nobody appears ever to have asked what it means.

30 The assumption is that the landscape is our living link with our history, the visible expression of our British roots, and that if we allow it to change ("to be destroyed", the conservationists would say), the link is broken forever. This view is palpably nonsensical. Our national identity is not defined by the landscape against which we carry on our lives. There is, in fact, no single thread that can be identified as our
35 rural heritage or tradition. Rather there is a bewildering array of different influences that have combined haphazardly through the centuries as successive invaders and immigrants and, later, successive generations, have reconstructed the landscape according to their own needs and ideas. What the conservationists seek to preserve is simply the landscape *as it is now*, in its incarnation of the early twenty-
40 first century. Far from affirming history, this approach actually denies it, for it would remove the continuous change without which history does not exist.

Where, for example, does the "traditional" landscape begin and end? If we take the period when the British Isles were born, nearly 8,000 years ago, we discover that the

45 conifers so hated by the conservationists today were one of the most important features of the scenery; the "English" oak and the much-loved elm were later immigrants from the warmer south. As for fauna, our "traditional" species included reindeer, rhinoceros, bison, hippopotamus and elephant. But where are they now?

Perhaps we should do better in the search for our heritage to consider what the countryside looked like when man first appeared in what we think of as Britain.
50 That would take us back 35,000 years, to the emergence of our ancestor *Homo sapiens*, who found himself in an Arctic landscape of ice and tundra. The remnants of that traditional scene can be found only in the highest mountains of Scotland; the rest of Britain has changed beyond recognition.

Obviously, then, we must look at more recent times if we are to discover identifiable
55 traditional elements in the landscape we now see about us. Yet if we do that, further difficulties emerge. The retreat of the last glaciation almost 11,000 years ago was accompanied by a relatively rapid warming of the climate, which gradually converted the open Arctic tundra into dense forest. This presented a serious challenge to Stone Age man, who began to find that the grazing animals, which he
60 hunted for food, were disappearing as their habitat retreated before the encroaching trees. In order to survive, he was forced to turn increasingly from hunting to farming, with the dramatic effects on flora and fauna that remain familiar to us today. As the quality of prehistoric tools improved, some stretches of forest were felled to provide grazing for domesticated animals, while grasses and cereals were
65 deliberately encouraged because of their usefulness to man. Even the shape of the countryside was changed as mining began to cut into hillsides, and in some places soil deterioration set in as the growing populations demanded perhaps the earliest form of intensive farming. In other words, the chief influence on the landscape of these islands was not nature but mankind.

PASSAGE 2

In the second passage, the journalist Richard Morrison responds to criticism of a Government plan to allow a million new houses to be built in southeast England.

PULLING UP THE DRAWBRIDGE

The English middle classes are rarely more hypocritical than when waxing indignant about "the threat to the countryside". What anguishes them usually turns out to be the threat to their own pleasure or to the value of their property. And I write those sentences with the heavy heart of a class traitor, for I am a
5 middle-class, middle-aged property owner who has smugly watched his own house soar in value as more and more young househunters desperately chase fewer and fewer properties. I am inordinately proud of my view across the green belt (from an upstairs window admittedly, because of the motorway flyover in between). And I intend to spend the weekend rambling across the rural England I have loved since
10 boyhood.

The most cherished credo of the English middle classes is that the verdant hills and dales of the Home Counties should remain forever sacrosanct, and that the Government's "Stalinist" decision to impose a million extra houses on southeast England is the most hideous threat to our way of life since the Luftwaffe made its
15 energetic contribution to British town and country planning in 1940. Thousands

of green acres will be choked by concrete, as rapacious housebuilders devour whole landscapes. England's cherished green belts—the 14 great rings of protected fields that have stopped our major cities from sprawling outward for more than half a century—will be swept away.

20 Yet if you sweep away the apoplectic froth and the self-interested posturing and look at the reality, the "threat to the countryside" recedes dramatically. Yes, we do occupy a crowded little island. But what makes it seem crowded is that 98 per cent of us live on 7 per cent of the land. Britain is still overwhelmingly green. Just 11 per cent of our nation is classified as urban.

25 Moreover, planners reckon that as much as a quarter of the green belt around London is wasteland, largely devoid of landscape beauty. So why not use it to relieve the intolerable pressure on affordable housing in the capital? Because that would contravene the long-held myth that green belts are vital "lungs" for cities. Well, lungs they might be. But they benefit chiefly those who live in nice houses 30 inside the green belts (not least by keeping their property values sky-high); and then those who live in nice houses in the leafy outer suburbs; and not at all the people who need the fresh air most: those on inner-city estates.

The green-belt protectionists claim to be saving unspoilt countryside from the rampant advance of bulldozers. Exactly what unspoilt countryside do they imagine 35 they are saving? Primordial forest, unchanged since Boadicea thrashed the Romans? Hogwash. The English have been making and remaking their landscape for millennia to suit the needs of each passing generation.

These protectionists are fond of deriding any housebuilding targets set by the Government as monstrous, Soviet-style diktats. Good grief, what on earth do they 40 imagine that the planning laws protecting green belts and agricultural land are, if not Government interventions that have had a huge, and often disastrous, impact not just on the property market, but on employment, on transport, on public services and on economic growth?

And, of course, on homelessness. Every time a bunch of middle-class homeowners 45 fights off the "intrusion" of a new housing estate into their cherished landscape, they make it more difficult for the young and the poor to find somewhere to live in reasonable proximity to where they can find work. This is the 21st-century equivalent of pulling up the drawbridge after one's own family and friends are safely inside the castle.

[END OF TEXT]

X115/302

NATIONAL
QUALIFICATIONS
2008

THURSDAY, 15 MAY
9.00 AM – 10.30 AM

ENGLISH
HIGHER
Close Reading–Questions

Answer all questions. **Use your own words whenever possible and particularly when you are instructed to do so.**

50 marks are allocated to this paper.

A code letter (U, A, E) is used alongside each question to give some indication of the skills being assessed. The number of marks attached to each question will give some indication of the length of answer required.

Questions on Passage 1 *Marks* *Code*

1. Read lines 1–7.

   Explain in your own words why the writer seems surprised that there is so much coverage of the "countryside debate". (line 1) 2 U

2. (a) Show how the word choice **and** sentence structure in lines 8–14 emphasise the strong feelings of those who feel the countryside is under threat. 4 A

   (b) Show how the writer's use of language in lines 15–20 conveys his disapproval of the "action groups". 2 A

3. Read lines 21–29.

   (a) By referring to specific words or phrases, show how lines 21–24 perform a linking function at this stage in the writer's argument. 2 U

   (b) Referring to lines 25–29, explain in your own words what the writer believes to be a "particularly worrying aspect of the new rural mania" (line 23). 2 U

4. "This view is palpably nonsensical." (lines 32–33)

   (a) Explain, using your own words as far as possible, what "this view" is. Refer to lines 30–32 in your answer. 2 U

   (b) Give in your own words **one** of the writer's reasons in lines 33–38 (". . . ideas.") for believing that the view is "palpably nonsensical". 2 U

   (c) Show how the writer's use of language in lines 38–41 reinforces his criticism of the conservationists' ideas. 2 A

5. Read lines 42–53.

   Give, in your own words as far as possible, any **three** reasons why it is difficult to define the "traditional" British landscape. 3 U

6. "This presented a serious challenge to Stone Age man . . ." (lines 58–59)

   (a) Explain in your own words what the "challenge" was. Refer to lines 54–61 (". . . trees.") in your answer. 2 U

   (b) Explain in your own words how Stone Age man responded to the challenge. Refer to lines 61–69 in your answer. 2 U

   (25)

	Marks	Code

Questions on Passage 2

7. (*a*) By referring to lines 1–3, explain in your own words why the writer believes that the English middle classes are being "hypocritical". **2** **U**

    (*b*) Show how the writer's use of language in lines 4–10 creates a self-mocking tone. **2** **A**

8. Show how the writer's use of language in lines 11–19 emphasises the extreme nature of the English middle classes' view of the threat to the countryside.

In your answer you should refer to specific language features such as: imagery, word choice, register . . . **4** **A**

9. Show how the writer's sentence structure **or** word choice in lines 20–24 emphasises his view that the threat to the countryside is much less serious than the English middle classes suggest. **2** **A**

10. (*a*) According to lines 25–27, why does the writer believe "a quarter of the green belt around London" should be used for housing? **2** **U**

    (*b*) How does the writer's use of language in lines 27 ("Because . . .") –32 cast doubt on the belief that green belts benefit everyone? **2** **A**

11. In lines 33–43 the writer criticises two further arguments put forward by the "green-belt protectionists".

Choose **either** the argument discussed in lines 33–37 **or** the argument discussed in lines 38–43, and answer **both** of the following questions on the paragraph you have chosen.

    (*a*) Explain why, in the writer's opinion, the green-belt protectionists' argument is flawed. **2** **U**

    (*b*) How effective do you find the writer's use of language in conveying his attitude to their argument? **2** **A/E**

12. How effective do you find lines 44–49 as a conclusion to the writer's attack on the attitudes of "middle-class homeowners"? **2** **E**

(20)

Question on both Passages

13. In Passage 1 David Sinclair refers to the claims of conservationists as "palpably nonsensical" and in Passage 2 Richard Morrison states that their views are "hogwash". Which writer is more successful in convincing you that these conservationists' claims are seriously flawed?

Justify your choice by referring to the **ideas and/or style** of **both passages**. **5** **E**

(5)

Total (50)

[END OF QUESTION PAPER]

[BLANK PAGE]

X115/303

NATIONAL
QUALIFICATIONS
2008

THURSDAY, 15 MAY
10.50 AM – 12.20 PM

ENGLISH
HIGHER
Critical Essay

Answer **two** questions.

Each question must be taken from a different section.

Each question is worth 25 marks.

Answer TWO questions from this paper. Each question must be chosen from a different Section (A–E). You are not allowed to choose two questions from the same Section.

In all Sections you may use Scottish texts.

Write the number of each question in the margin of your answer booklet and begin each essay on a fresh page.

You should spend about 45 minutes on each essay.

The following will be assessed:

- the relevance of your essays to the questions you have chosen, and the extent to which you sustain an appropriate line of thought

- your knowledge and understanding of key elements, central concerns and significant details of the chosen texts, supported by detailed and relevant evidence

- your understanding, as appropriate to the questions chosen, of how relevant aspects of structure/style/language contribute to the meaning/effect/impact of the chosen texts, supported by detailed and relevant evidence

- your evaluation, as appropriate to the questions chosen, of the effectiveness of the chosen texts, supported by detailed and relevant evidence

- the quality of your written expression and the technical accuracy of your writing.

SECTION A—DRAMA

Answers to questions on drama should address relevantly the central concern(s)/theme(s) of the text and be supported by reference to appropriate dramatic techniques such as: conflict, characterisation, key scene(s), dialogue, climax, exposition, dénouement, structure, plot, setting, aspects of staging (such as lighting, music, stage set, stage directions . . .), soliloquy, monologue . . .

1. Choose a play in which a central character is heroic yet vulnerable.

   Show how the dramatist makes you aware of both qualities and discuss how they affect your response to the character's fate in the play as a whole.

2. Choose a play which explores the theme of love in difficult circumstances.

   Explain how the dramatist introduces the theme and discuss how in the course of the play he/she prepares you for the resolution of the drama.

3. Choose from a play a scene in which an important truth is revealed.

   Briefly explain what the important truth is and assess the significance of its revelation to your understanding of theme or character.

4. Choose a play in which a character has to exist in a hostile environment.

   Briefly describe the environment and discuss the extent to which it influences your response to the character's behaviour and to the outcome of the play.

SECTION B—PROSE

Prose Fiction

> *Answers to questions on prose fiction should address relevantly the central concern(s)/theme(s) of the text(s) and be supported by reference to appropriate techniques of prose fiction such as: characterisation, setting, key incident(s), narrative technique, symbolism, structure, climax, plot, atmosphere, dialogue, imagery . . .*

5. Choose a **novel** which explores the cruelty of human nature.

   Show how the writer explores this theme and discuss how its exploration enhances your appreciation of the novel as a whole.

6. Choose a **novel** in which a confrontation between two characters is of central importance in the text.

   Explain the circumstances of the confrontation and discuss its importance to your understanding of the novel as a whole.

7. Choose **two short stories** which you appreciated because of the surprising nature of their endings.

   Compare the techniques used in creating these surprising endings and discuss which ending you feel is more successful as a conclusion.

8. Choose a **novel** or **short story** which is set during a period of social or political change.

   Discuss how important the writer's evocation of the period is to your appreciation of the text as a whole.

Prose Non-fiction

> *Answers to questions on prose non-fiction should address relevantly the central concern(s)/theme(s) of the text and be supported by reference to appropriate techniques of prose non-fiction such as: ideas, use of evidence, selection of detail, point of view, stance, setting, anecdote, narrative voice, style, language, structure, organisation of material . . .*

9. Choose a **non-fiction text** which you consider inspiring or provocative.

   Explain how the writer's presentation of his/her subject has such an impact on you.

10. Choose a piece of **travel writing** which offers surprising or amusing insights into a particular country or culture.

    Explain briefly what you learn about the country or culture and in greater detail discuss the techniques the writer uses to surprise or amuse you.

11. Choose a **non-fiction text** in which you consider the writer's stance on a particular issue to be ambiguous.

    Show how the writer's presentation of this issue illustrates the ambiguity of her/his stance.

[Turn over

SECTION C—POETRY

Answers to questions on poetry should address relevantly the central concern(s)/theme(s) of the text(s) and be supported by reference to appropriate poetic techniques such as: imagery, verse form, structure, mood, tone, sound, rhythm, rhyme, characterisation, contrast, setting, symbolism, word choice . . .

12. Choose a poem which deals with conflict or danger or death.

    Show how the poet creates an appropriate mood for the subject matter and go on to discuss how effectively she/he uses this mood to enhance your understanding of the central idea of the poem.

13. Choose a poem which is strongly linked to a specific location.

    Show how the poet captures the essence of the location and exploits this to explore an important theme.

14. Choose **two** poems which explore human relationships.

    By referring to both poems, discuss which you consider to be the more convincing portrayal of a relationship.

15. Choose a poem in which the speaker's personality is gradually revealed.

    Show how, through the content and language of the poem, aspects of the character gradually emerge.

SECTION D—FILM AND TV DRAMA

Answers to questions on film and TV drama should address relevantly the central concern(s)/theme(s) of the text(s) and be supported by reference to appropriate techniques of film and TV drama such as: key sequence(s), characterisation, conflict, structure, plot, dialogue, editing/montage, sound/soundtrack, aspects of mise-en-scène (such as lighting, colour, use of camera, costume, props . . .), mood, setting, casting, exploitation of genre . . .

16. Choose a **film** or **TV drama*** in which a particular sequence is crucial to your understanding of an important theme.

    By referring to the sequence and to the text as a whole, show why you consider the sequence to be so important to your understanding of the theme.

17. Choose a **film** or **TV drama*** which presents a life-affirming story.

    By referring to key elements of the text, show how the story has such an effect.

18. Choose a **film** or **TV drama*** in which intense feelings have tragic consequences.

    Show to what extent the film or programme makers' presentation of these feelings and their consequences is successful in engaging you with the text.

19. Choose a **film** or **TV drama*** in which a complex character is revealed.

    Show how the film or programme makers reveal the complexity and discuss to what extent this aspect of the character contributes to your response to the text.

*"TV drama" includes a single play, a series or a serial.

[Turn over

SECTION E—LANGUAGE

Answers to questions on language should address relevantly the central concern(s) of the language research/study and be supported by reference to appropriate language concepts such as: register, jargon, tone, vocabulary, word choice, technical terminology, presentation, illustration, accent, grammar, idiom, slang, dialect, structure, point of view, orthography, abbreviation . . .

20. Consider uses of language designed to interest you in a social or commercial or political campaign.

Identify aspects of language which you feel are intended to influence you and evaluate their success in raising your awareness of the subject of the campaign.

21. Consider the spoken language of a clearly defined group of people.

Identify features which differentiate this language from standard usage and assess the extent to which these features have useful functions within the group.

22. Consider the language of newspaper reporting on such subjects as fashion, celebrities, reality TV, soap stars. . .

Identify some of the characteristics of this language and discuss to what extent it is effective in communicating with its target audience.

23. Consider the language (written and/or symbolic) associated with the use of e-mails or text messaging or instant messaging.

Describe some of the conventions associated with any one of these and discuss to what extent these conventions lead to more effective communication.

[END OF QUESTION PAPER]

[BLANK PAGE]

Official SQA Past Papers: Higher English 2008

[BLANK PAGE]

[BLANK PAGE]

[BLANK PAGE]

[BLANK PAGE]

Acknowledgements

Leckie and Leckie is grateful to the copyright holders, as credited, for permission to use their material:

The article 'Protective Parents, yes, But Paranoid?' by Catherine Bennett © Guardian Newspapers Ltd 2001 (2004 Close Reading p 3);

Impact! The Threat of Comets and Asteroids by Gerrit L Verschur, copyright © 1996 by Gerrit L Verschur. Used by permission of Oxford University Press, Inc. (2005 Higher pp 2-3);

The article 'Asteroid Could Blast Us Back To Dark Ages' 3 September 2003, taken from The Mirror © Mirrorpix (2005 Close Reading pp 3-4);

The Economist for the article 'The Shape of Things to Come' 18 December 2003, taken from K www.economist.com (2006 Close Reading pp 2-3);

The Scotsman for the article 'Despite Google, we still need good libraries' by George Kerevan (2007 Close Reading pp 2-3);

The Times for the article 'Paradise is paper, parchment and dust' by Ben Macintyre © NI Syndication (2007 Close Reading pp 3-4);

The Times for an article 'Yes, I will let Mr Prescott build in my Backyard' by Richard Morrison © NI Syndication (2008 Close Reading pp3-4).

The following companies have very generously given permission to reproduce their copyright material free of charge:

The article 'Is paranoid Parenting the Greatest Danger to our Kids?' by Melanie Reid courtesy of The Herald © Newsquest Media Group (2004 Close Reading p 2);

The Guardian & Observer for the article 'Foolish Panic is about Profit' by Susie Orbach (2006 Close Reading p 4).

English Higher
Close Reading
2007

Questions on Passage 1

1. (a) Acceptable gloss on 'ecstatic': e.g. joyous, thrilled, excited, delighted …; 'happy' by itself is not acceptable: there must be some idea of intensity

Acceptable gloss on 'nostalgic': e.g. looking back fondly, wistful, regretful, reflective, … 'sad/unhappy' by itself not acceptable: there must be some idea of something connected with past OR the idea that he is apprehensive, fearful (at possible loss/demise of libraries)

(b) *Possible answers:*
1. 'book-lined' suggests large number/area of books, implying organised, impressive nature…
2. 'cathedral-quiet' has connotations of solemnity, reverence, devotion, large hushed space…
3. 'cherished' suggests cared for emotionally (rather than just practically), warmth…
4. 'civilisation' has connotations of that which marks us out from less sophisticated societies
5. 'lose' has a sense of being deprived, bereft…
6. 'cultural' suggests traditions, heritage, civilised society,…
7. 'peril' suggests threat, risk, menace, danger (to something precious)

2. *Possible answers:*

'High priority':
1. Use of 'remembered' suggests that the library, although initially overlooked, was indeed a priority.
2. Despite the fact they 'neglected shops and amenities', they still put in a library, which suggests that it was considered more important than these.

'Low priority':
3. The high number (60,000) of potential users contrasted with the smallness of the facility (a 'shed') suggests inadequacy.
4. Use of 'remembered' suggests it was an afterthought, a last-minute idea.
5. The fact it was a 'wooden shed' suggests it was basic, cheap, unsophisticated, temporary and therefore considered of little importance.
6. The use of 'somehow' indicates that nobody was sure why the decision had been taken; it just happened.
7. The tone of '– actually, a wooden shed' as if a rather amused, sarcastic aside suggests an afterthought, a wry admission of its inadequacies.

3. *Possible answers:*

Imagery:
1. 'stretching'
   gives the impression of something being pulled or elongated with connotations of never-ending, upward movement, aspiring
2. 'cocooned'
   as larvae are protected and self-contained in their cocoons, so each floor in the library is separate and shelters the students within their specialised knowledge areas
3. 'worlds of knowledge'
   the number of floors is so great and they are so separate that they are like different, independent planetary systems, each specialising in a particular area of knowledge
4. 'planets'
   the separation into large, distinct learning areas, each self-contained like the isolation and individualism of each planet in space

Word choice:
5. 'wonder'
   connotations of awe, freshness, childlike amazement, admiration …
6. 'skyscraper (library)'
   slightly exaggerated description suggests size and magnificence (be sympathetic to candidates who choose to see 'skyscraper' as an image)
7. 'vast'
   gives the impression of an enormous extent of space
8. 'atrium'
   idea of large, impressive central area – with connotations of classical ideas/ learning
9. 'devoted'
   connotations of love, reverence, dedication
10. 'chatting, flirting, doodling, panicking' (any of these)
    suggestions of human foibles, ordinary behaviour <u>contrasted with the extraordinary nature of the library</u>
11. 'exploring'
    suggests excitement of new discovery, sense of quest, hint of size,…
12. 'unique'
    suggestions of something very special, to be marvelled at …

N.B. words from 1–4 above could be the subject of appropriate comments as word choice.

4. (a) *Possible answers:*

Sentence structure:
1. The climactic nature of the second sentence: builds up from an abrupt start to the negative attitude by 'chatter…at a thousand decibels' **or** (possibly) presents a positive attitude in admiring their ability to communicate loudly or their ability to carry out more than one task at a time.

English Higher
Close Reading
2007 (cont.)

4. (*a*)   2. Use of questions could suggest a positive attitude by backing up the idea that young people are modern and that they do not approve of subsidising libraries **or** combined with a mock-scornful tone could suggest that he believes the answer to the questions is that we do need libraries rather than the slick media world of the MTV generation – ie a negative attitude.

3. Structure of the first sentence: a case might just be made that the colon is used to introduce a demonstration of the writer's attitude that he prefers the past to the present and therefore will be critical of the MTV generation.

Word choice:

4. 'multi-tasking' suggests positive attitude in that these people are seen as talented in their ability to perform several tasks simultaneously **or** suggests a negative attitude in that in trying to do so many things at once, due attention is not given to the important matters.

5. 'cheap books' suggests positive aspects in that these books are readily available to all without recourse to a library **or** negatively, the books are cheap in the sense of not worth much intellectually.

6. 'chatter' is negative in that the word suggests inconsequential communication **or** positive in that it suggests easy personal interaction.

7. 'thousand decibels' probably negative in that it suggests that the noise is too loud for real thought.

8. 'old-fashioned' is probably negative in that it suggests he thinks the MTV generation is too readily dismissive, or too keen to believe libraries are outdated.

Tone:

9. derogatory (backed up by any of the comments suggested above)

10. admiring (backed up by any of the comments suggested above)

11. mock-scornful/sarcastic (backed up by any of the comments suggested above)

(*b*) A basic understanding that diminishing use of libraries leads to diminishing levels of provision, which leads to diminishing use …

5. (*a*) *Any four of the following:*

1. idea of accessibility (i.e. acceptable gloss on 'strategically situated')

2. idea of free access (i.e. acceptable gloss on 'too expensive … to buy')

3. idea that resources are more sophisticated (i.e. acceptable gloss on 'too complex to find online')

5. (*a*) continued

4. idea of supporting democratic responsibilities (i.e. acceptable gloss on 'informed citizenship')

5. idea of community awareness/cohesion (i.e. acceptable gloss on 'civic pride')

6. idea of professional support (i.e. acceptable gloss on 'trained librarian')

7. idea of informed/refined selection (i.e. acceptable gloss on 'honed and developed by experts')

8. idea of high standard of material (i.e. acceptable gloss on 'quality … of information')

9. idea of authenticity (i.e. acceptable gloss on 'veracity of information')

10. idea of selectivity of information (in contrast with junk online)

(*b*) For libraries, answers should make acceptable comment on the positive connotations of any of the following:
'trained'
'honed'
'developed'
'experts'
'guarantee'
'quality'
'veracity'

For the internet, answers should make acceptable comment on the negative connotations of any of the following:
'Achilles' heel'
'(of course) nonsense'
'cluttered'
'false'
'(plain) junk'
'never'

6. (*a*) Any acceptable gloss, e.g. guardians, protectors, those who keep something safe, …

(*b*) *Possible answers:*

Word choice:

1. '(become the) fashion' has connotations of transience, shallowness, …

2. 'entertainment centres'/'audio-visuals' has connotations of pandering to popular taste, lack of seriousness, …

3. 'gimmicks' has connotations of cheap trickery, merely to capture attention, …

4. 'popularising' has connotations of dumbing down, aiming for lowest common denominator, …

5. 'reduced' has connotations of loss of quality, depth, sophistication, …

6. 'child's view' has connotations of naiveté, lack of sophistication, limited perspective, …

Tone:

7 grudging: 'some (enthusiasm)' suggests reluctance to welcome the idea fully

8 scornful: appropriate comment based on any of 1–6 above

6. (*b*) (continued)

    9. didactic: appropriate comment on lines 52–54 ('cannot always be reduced', 'duty', 'future generations', 'invest', 'culture')

Structure:

  10. The list ('audio-visuals, interactive displays and gimmicks'), ending in the anti-climax ('gimmicks'), reduces the other items to meaningless technical tricks.

  11. The structure of 'While I have … universe' is a limited concession which emphasises the dismissiveness of what follows.

7. *Possible answers:*

Ideas:

    1. Google and the Bodleian Library are brought together again in this paragraph.

    2. The idea of large numbers (one million books) on Google/the vastness of libraries leading to an understanding of the enormous amount of material which can never be known.

    3. The differentiation between information and wisdom is what the passage has been leading up to.

Language:

    4. 'Of course' may be a strategic concession/ idea of bringing reader onside/of being reasonable – in preparation for conclusion.

    5. 'Yet here's' conversational tone leads the reader to come on board and share his ideas.

    6. 'daunting' is a strong word suggesting the enormous and frightening amount of knowledge.

    7. 'even a fraction' suggests, in contrast, the very small proportion with which one person can come to grips.

    8. 'Ever.' This emphatic, one word sentence closes the door on the possibility of conquering all knowledge.

    9. 'merely imbibing' In contrast with wisdom, this suggests that information acquired simply as quantity, without understanding or context, is as mechanical as drinking.

  10. Word order in last sentence: the inversion of normal order places the realisation very close to the 'ever' which gives it more impact, and leaves the important word 'wisdom' to follow its verb and take a central place in the last sentence

  11. Dash plus final statement in last sentence: the pause created by the dash puts emphasis on the last words ('merely imbibing information'), throwing them into stronger contrast with 'the beginning of wisdom' which is the thrust of the passage as a whole.

Questions on Passage 2

8. (*a*) *Any one of the following:*

    1. (very) happy

    2. idyllic

    3. carefree

    4. nostalgic

    5. calm, peaceful

    6. any other answer which conveys a positive feeling or the importance of the memory to the writer

(*b*) *Possible answers:*

    1. 'We are surrounded by eight million books.' The very short, declarative, unembellished sentence emphasises the simple, breathtaking fact.

    2. 'eight million books' gives an overwhelming sense of quantity.

    3. 'on every side' is awe-inspiring because the books are inescapable, almost intimidating.

    4. 'hundreds of yards deep' shows the sheer scale of the collection.

    5. 'at the rate of two miles a year' conveys the impressive growth rate.

    6. 'surrounded by', 'Behind', 'beneath': these directional details and the use of a variety of prepositions and adverbial phrases of place convey the omnipresence of books.

    7. 'reach into the sky' conveys the idea of towering beyond the normal, aspirational, connotations of heavenly, …

    8. '(in compact) ranks' gives an image of armed forces which suggests the highly organised positioning of the books.

    9. 'subterranean' conveys a sense of dark, mysterious, alluring.

  10. 'subterranean stacks': the alliteration suggests hushed reverence.

  11. 'entombed in words'. This image of burial suggests the all-encompassing presence of books.

  12. 'unimaginable (volume)': beyond the power of the mind to conceive

  13. 'cold storage' conveys a sci-fi idea of some potential waiting to be revived.

  14. 'quiet and vast and waiting': this climactic description suggests the overpowering, slightly menacing, nature of such an enormous collection.

(*c*) *Possible answer:*

The repetition of 'perhaps' conveys the writer's wistful uncertainty and makes the reader aware that he has a wealth of happy memories from which to choose.

English Higher
Close Reading
2007 (cont.)

9. Possible comments:
    1. 'temple': just as a temple is a place of worship and reverence, a library deserves our utmost respect (because of the accumulation of knowledge which it contains).
    2. 'core': just as the core is the heart, the essential part, a library is central to our lives and society.
    3. 'citadel': just as a citadel is a fortress, a library provides a stronghold to safeguard all that we consider most precious.

10. (a) It could signal the end of conventional libraries, (which will no longer be used), i.e. a basic understanding of 'could finally destroy traditional libraries, which will become mere warehouses for the physical objects, empty of people and life' (lines 28-30).

    (b) *Any three of the following:*
    1. A single catalogue will ensure that everything is stored in one place.
    2. Democracy – knowledge will be available to all.
    3. It will be impossible to wipe out knowledge (by destroying books).
    4. Totalitarian states will not be able to keep knowledge to themselves/deny it to the masses.

11. (a) *Either or both of the following (mark will depend on clarity of explanation):*
    1. There is visual beauty in the book itself.
    2. There is sensual pleasure in holding the actual book.

    (b) *Any one or more of the following:*
    1. acceptable gloss on 'central to our understanding of what it is to be human' – libraries allow us to find out about life and our position in it
    2. acceptable gloss on 'sociable thinking, exploring and exchanging ideas' – function of libraries as a meeting place for discussion
    3. acceptable gloss on 'recreational' – libraries as places of relaxation or even romance

12. *Example answers:*

    Ideas:
    1. The film illustrates the conflict between libraries and new technology - the two main characters represent the two sides
    2. The passage ends on a positive note - libraries and online catalogue can happily co-exist

12. *Example answers: (cont.)*

    Language/Style:
    3. literal and metaphorical marriage
    4. 'smooching': jocular, informal reference to easy, affectionate, slightly old-fashioned relationship
    5. play on words: 'everyone reads happily ever after'
    6. The single sentence final paragraph sums up the link between the film and the co-existence of libraries and an online catalogue.

Questions on both Passages

13. The mark for this question will reflect the overall quality of the response and may not be directly related to the length of response or to the number of points/references made. A succinct, sophisticated response will be worth more than a series of fairly trivial points and obvious references.

    For full marks there must be a reference to both elements (i.e. ideas and style) and to both passages (although not necessarily a balanced treatment) and convincing evaluative comment.
    1. Some candidates may choose to argue that the passages are equally persuasive, focusing in (part of) their answers on similarities in ideas, style and length. This could be a legitimate approach and such answers should be judged on their merits.
    2. Some candidates may make use of the writers' criticisms of the internet to imply support for libraries. This is broadly acceptable, provided it contributes effectively to a line of thought about the writers' views.

    Some of the points listed below could be made:

    Ideas – Passage 1:
    • libraries are a part of civilisation
    • libraries aid learning
    • libraries as a physical space can have an important/positive impact on people
    • libraries allow shared learning experiences
    • libraries allow people to socialise
    • libraries encourage people to explore other areas of knowledge
    • libraries allow easy and affordable access to books/knowledge
    • librarians offer vital expertise
    • libraries are user-friendly
    • (as opposed to the internet) people can have confidence in the authenticity/validity/reliability of material in libraries
    • libraries safeguard important books/documents/materials
    • libraries as a physical space emphasise the extent of human knowledge

13. (continued)

Ideas – Passage 2:
- libraries encourage young people's interest in reading
- libraries are linked to civilised values
- libraries make the acquisition of knowledge a sociable activity
- libraries are symbolic representations of civilisation/knowledge/man's finer points
- libraries allow easy access to books as physical objects (which the writer thinks is important)
- people are reading more books than ever
- (however, libraries are vulnerable guardians of knowledge)

Style – Passage 1:
- use of varied personal memories as platform for ideas/observations
- detailed, evocative use of language to convey love of libraries
- variation in tone to match flow of argument (humorous, nostalgic, assertive, dismissive, conversational, etc)
- use of statistics
- forceful ending to stress importance of ideas

Style – Passage 2:
- use of varied personal memories as platform for ideas/observations
- use of sensual language to convey emotional nature of engagement
- use of various stylistic devices to convey his awe/reverence for libraries (facts and figures; extended imagery; accumulative style)
- use of historical perspective to contextualise the importance and evolving nature of libraries
- use of humour, especially in the rather playful ending

English Higher
Critical Essay
2007

Please refer to the answer guidelines for the Critical Essay in the English Higher 2006.

English Higher
Close Reading 2008

1. 1. gloss on "one could be forgiven for thinking that we still live in small peasant communities dependent upon the minutest shift in agricultural policy" – idea that we are still a rural society affected by farming laws

    and/or

    2. gloss on "it has seemed almost as if we were still in the early nineteenth century when we relied on the countryside to survive" – as if we were still living in the past when we were more rurally dependent

2. (a) Possible answers:

    Word choice:
    1. "cried constantly"
        suggests a state of permanent outrage
    2. "mortal danger"
        suggests extreme peril, life-threatening
    3. "greedy"
        suggests they are over-eager for monetary gain
    4. "only motive is profit"
        suggests single-minded quest for gain
    5. "kept on roaring"
        suggests persistent expression of anger, aggression
    6. "killing every wild thing in sight"
        use of hyperbole to express scale of destruction
    7. "threatening the very soil"
        intensive, emphasising extent of menace
    8. "overuse"
        suggests injury by excessive use
    9. "continually … ululating"
        suggests constant loud lamentations

    Sentence structure:
    10. listing (lines 12-14)
        emphasises the range of alternatives which provoke protest
    11. repetition of "or"
        suggests determination to find a source of complaint
    12. Tripartite structure of "One faction has cried", "another has kept on roaring" and "still another … ululating" in three sections separated by semi-colons building to a climax of noisy dissent.

    (b) Possible answers:

    Word choice:
    1. "proliferation"
        suggests excessive increase in numbers
    2. "dedicated"
        suggests obsessiveness, misplaced devotion
    3. "multifarious"
        suggests an inappropriate or confusing variety

2. (b) continued
    4. "have become accustomed"
        suggests force of habit rather than genuine concern
    5. "expending"
        suggests consumption to little purpose
    6. "their time and energies"
        suggests an all-consuming obsession
    7. "countless other aspects"
        suggests needless involvement in every area

    Sentence structure:
    8. list of features (lines 15-16)
        range of objections conveys excessive nature of protests
    9. list of projects (lines 18-20)
        excessive concern about a wide range of aspects of nature

    Tone:
    10. "moorlands, uplands, lowlands"
        dismissive tone – as if "any old lands"
    11. any of 1-9 above could be discussed in terms of a dismissive, scathing, contemptuous tone

3. (a) 1. "returned to the central position" refers to the aim of the action groups mentioned in lines 15-20 (no credit for the quotation unless the reference back is identified)
        2. "worrying aspect" points forward to concerns the writer has (no credit for the quotation unless the reference forward is identified)

    (b) 1. acceptable gloss on "identification . . . of the countryside in general and the landscape in particular with the past", eg that rural features are the only way of understanding our history
        2. desire to preserve what is perceived as "our heritage"
        3. difficulty in defining what is meant by the term "our heritage"

4. (a) 1. acceptable gloss on "our living link with our history" eg tangible, actual, real, visible connection with the past
        2. acceptable gloss on "the visible expression of our British roots" eg outward display, evidence of our heritage, identity
        3. failure to preserve the landscape will cause the connection to be lost

    (b) *Any two from:*
        1. who we are by race, our sense of belonging, does not stem from the physical setting in which we live
        2. there is no one connecting link between the countryside of today and the countryside of the past
        3. many diverse influences have joined to create a landscape which has suited the creators' own purposes

4. (*c*) Possible answers:
  1. "simply"
     pejorative, reductive view
  2. "*as it is now*"
     use of italics stresses the conservationists' total rejection of change
  3. beginning sentence "Far from affirming history"
     emphasises mistaken approach
  4. "affirming", "denies"
     juxtaposition of opposites reinforces the weakness of the conservationists' position
  5. "actually"
     reinforces the contrast between affirmation and denial
  6. "the continuous change without which history does not exist"
     final climactic assertion of writer's belief in direct opposition to the ideas of the conservationists

5. *Any three from:*
  1. it is impossible to define a point in time for the start of "tradition"
  2. conifers, which are unpopular nowadays, were significant in the past
  3. our more iconic species of trees (oak and elm) arrived much later
  4. animals (reindeer, rhinoceros, bison, hippopotamus, elephant) which have now vanished used to be abundant
  5. when man first appeared in Britain, the landscape was Arctic ice and tundra

6. (*a*) *Any two from:*
  1. hunting became more difficult …
  2. … as the grazing animals started to die out/became difficult to find …
  3. … because of increased afforestation

  (*b*) *Any two from:*
  1. Stone Age man relied more on farming than on hunting
  2. he improved the efficiency of his farming tools
  3. he created space for grasslands for animals and/or crops
  4. crops were increasingly grown to serve man's needs

7. (*a*) the middle classes are not really worried about the countryside; what really concerns them is: gloss on "(the threat to) their own pleasure" or on "(the threat to) the value of their own property"

  (*b*) Possible answers:
  1. "heavy heart" deliberate exaggeration of the extent of his remorse
  2. "class traitor" inflated description suggesting his opinions constitute some terrible act/betrayal

7. (*b*) continued

  3. "middle-class, middle-aged property owner"
     writer deliberately casts himself as an archetype, clichéd representative of his class
  4. "smugly watched"
     suggests the writer is complacent, self-satisfied, gloating
  5. "soar in value"
     suggests a smug belief that his own success is both effortless and impressive
  6. "inordinately proud"
     suggests a pride which is hard to justify, excessive, out of all proportion
  7. "my view"
     suggests smug possessiveness
  8. "from an upstairs window"
     lampoons/undercuts the writer's pride in his view by suggesting the view is limited, inaccessible, awkward…
  9. "motorway flyover in between"
     suggests something man-made, ugly, functional – ridiculing the writer's pride in his view
  10. parenthesis (lines 7-8)
     apparently a throwaway qualification, but in reality used by the writer to highlight the overblown nature of his pride/undercut his argument
  11. repetition of "(And) I" at the start of sentences suggests self-absorbed, egotistical, pompous nature of middle classes
  12. repetition of "I" followed by active verb suggests an inflated belief in the importance of his actions/opinions
  13. contrast the ghastliness of his self-satisfied pride ("smugly watched", "soar in value") is heightened by the contrast with the desperation of the "young househunters" (In developing this point candidates might comment on the balance of "more and more"/"fewer and fewer".)

8. Possible answers:

  Imagery:
  1. "cherished credo"
     A "credo" is a religious belief. This suggests the reverence and/or depth of the middle classes' devotion to the countryside.
  2. "forever sacrosanct"
     Something "sacrosanct" is sacred and untouchable. This implies an almost religious conviction that the countryside should remain unaltered, suggests the countryside is holy ground and changing it would be sacrilegious.
  3. " 'Stalinist' decision"
     Stalin is considered to be an oppressive, ruthless dictator. This portrays the Government as dictatorial, evil, brutal, cruel, heartless …

English Higher
Close Reading
2008 (cont.)

8. continued

    4. "choked (by concrete)"
       Being "choked" involves strangulation, difficulty in breathing. This suggests the countryside is being destroyed, having the life squeezed out of it, unable to flourish, under attack.

    5. "rapacious housebuilders"
       A "rapacious" act is a predatory one involving, for example, a bird of prey. This suggests the builders are aggressive, plundering, greedy, self-interested, voracious, gluttonous...

    6. "devour whole landscapes"
       To "devour" something is to eat it up greedily. This suggests the builders are greedy, insatiable, all-consuming, indiscriminate...

    7. "sprawling outward"
       To "sprawl" is to sit or lie in an awkward, ungainly way. This suggests the outward movement of the cities would be haphazard, unattractive, disorderly...

    8. "will be swept away"
       "swept away" could refer to brushing or tidal movement. Either way, it suggests a rapid, extensive, conclusive end to the green belts.

Word choice:

    9. "verdant hills and dales"
       idealised, Eden-like vision of the countryside as lush, fertile

   10. "forever"
       intensifies belief in inviolable nature of the countryside

   11. "impose"
       suggests compulsion, force, authoritarian government

   12. "most hideous"
       superlatively repulsive, despicable, morally offensive

   13. "threat"
       suggests pain, injury, a menacing, bullying enemy...

   14. "our way of life"
       suggests a set of shared, traditional, important values

   15. "since the Luftwaffe ... in 1940"
       (comparing the effect of more houses to the damage caused by German bombers) suggests they fear huge destruction, regard the builders as an evil, destructive, aggressive enemy

   16. "cherished green belts"
       the countryside is loved and treasured

   17. "14 great rings"
       majestic, impressive, powerful, important

8. continued

   Register:

   18. candidates should be rewarded who make a sensible attempt to identify a register (inflated, over-the-top, exaggerated, mock-reverential, faux-outraged) and then – through appropriate reference and analysis – show how the writer's use of this register pokes fun at, attacks, exemplifies the views of the middle classes; any of the listed examples of imagery and word choice might be used to support such an answer

9. Possible answers:

   Sentence structure:

    1. the positioning of "Yet" at the start of the opening sentence sets up the rebuttal of the preceding argument

    2. contrast/balance in opening sentence of "sweep away"/"look at" moves argument forward

    3. structure of opening sentence places emphasis on principal clause at its conclusion

    4. short, (apparently) concessionary 2nd sentence, introduced by "Yes", is immediately qualified/contradicted by 3rd sentence

    5. positioning of "But" at start of 3rd sentence sets up qualification/contradiction to 2nd sentence

    6. repetition of "seem crowded" following "crowded" also underlines 3rd sentence's qualification/contradiction

    7. short, punchy, declarative final two sentences drive home writer's point

    8. positioning of "Just" at start of final sentence underlines (surprisingly small) statistic

    9. candidates may comment on the writer's general sign-posting at the start of sentences: "Yet", "Yes", "But", "Just" to flag up the oppositional nature of his argument

   Word choice:

   10. "sweep away"
       suggests previous argument is "rubbish" and can be dealt with/dismissed very quickly

   11. "apoplectic"
       suggests uncontrolled, irrational anger

   12. "froth"
       suggests something insubstantial, trivial...

   13. "self-interested"
       suggests middle classes only concerned with themselves, not the countryside

   14. "posturing"
       suggests middle classes' concern is exaggerated, contrived, fake, affected ...

   15. "look at the reality"
       suggests truth is clear and incontrovertible

   16. "recedes dramatically"
       suggests rapid movement, significant diminution of threat

9. continued

17. "overwhelmingly green"
emphasises full extent of Britain's rural make-up
18. "classified"
official nature of term reinforces accuracy, validity of statistic
19. use of personal pronouns ("you … we …us …our")
clear attempt to make the reader share his point of view/involve the reader personally

10. (a)   1. gloss on "wasteland, largely devoid of landscape beauty": eg it is a wilderness, it is not attractive, it serves no purpose, it has no redeeming features
and
2. there is a desperate shortage of housing in London (for reasons of space and/or cost)

(b) Possible answers:

Word choice
1. "myth"
suggests belief is untrue, fictitious, irrational, fanciful
2. "Well, lungs they might be"
suggests reluctant, grudging, conditional acceptance of claim
3. "not at all"
definitive, categorical negative

Sentence structure:
4. "Well, lungs they might be"
inversion places emphasis on writer's doubt/scepticism
5. "But"
position at start of sentence introduces idea of rebuttal
6. parenthesis (line 30)
used to point out slyly that the middle classes benefit commercially as well as environmentally
7. progressive nature of final sentence
using semi-colons, the writer divides final sentence into three sections to stress the diminishing benefits of green belts and/or
the diminishing benefits are also signposted structurally by the use of "chiefly", "and then" and "and not at all" at the start of each section
8. climax of final sentence
writer uses colon to introduce, direct attention to those who are not advantaged by green belts

Tone:
9. "Well, lungs they might be"
dismissive, sceptical tone stresses his lack of belief
10. "nice houses", "leafy suburbs"
use of clichés creates a rather mocking tone towards those enjoying a comfortable, carefree existence

10. (b) continued

11. "(not least … values sky-high)"
ironic aside underlines writer's scepticism towards middle classes

Other language features:
12. any other acceptable suggestion supported by appropriate reference and explanation

11. lines 33–37

(a) Possible answer:
green-belt protectionists believe they are protecting land which has been unchanged for centuries when in reality each generation has changed the land as required

(b) Possible answers:

Word choice:
1. "claim"
suggests doubt/dubiety
2. "rampant advance"
suggests insatiable demands; uses hyperbole to make their claims seem absurd, over the top, fanciful
3. "bulldozers" (used to symbolise builders)
connotations of indiscriminate destruction, demolition; again suggests protectionists' claims are deliberately exaggerated, alarmist
4. "exactly what"
suggests claims lack detail
5. "imagine"
suggests green-belt protectionists are removed from reality, living in a dream world
6. "Primordial forest", "Boadicea", "the Romans"
deliberate reference to very distant times/people stresses the unlikeliness of the green-belt campaigners' claims or implicit comparison of their claims to Boadicea's heroic life-or-death battle against a genuine aggressor highlights their pretension, self-importance, lack of perspective
7. "Hogwash"
categorical condemnation – claims are worthless, false, ridiculous, "garbage"
8. "making and remaking"
suggests change is ongoing, inevitable process

Sentence structure:
9. repetition of questions
hectoring, nagging, confrontational
10. single-word sentence
highlights his utter rejection of their claims
11. fluent, formal final sentence (in comparison to previous sentence)
controlled, certain, assured, rational

Tone:
12. scornful/dubious – "claim"
13. satirical – "rampant advance"

English Higher
Close Reading
2008 (cont.)

11. lines 33–37   (b) continued

   14. dismissive/incredulous – "exactly what", "imagine"

   15. humorous – "primordial", "Boadicea thrashed the Romans"

   16. dismissive, contemptuous – deliberate informality of "Hogwash"

   17. authoritative, certain – created by formality of final sentence (in contrast to the previous sentence)

11. lines 38–43

(a) Possible answers:

green-belt protectionists think the government is imposing change/being authoritarian but current planning laws are equally harsh/dictatorial

and/or

green-belt protectionists oppose the government's plans to build houses/change green belt planning but the existing planning laws have worked out poorly/been calamitous or are very protective of the countryside

(b) Possible answers:

Word choice:
   1. "fond"
      suggests green-belt protectionists are self-indulgent, enjoy being critical
   2. "deriding"
      suggests their arguments are cruel, contemptuous, destructive
   3. "monstrous"
      deliberate exaggeration to make their claims seem excessive
   4. "Soviet-style diktats"
      comparison to authoritarian state suggests green-belt protectionists' views are alarmist and excessive
   5. "imagine"
      suggests their ideas are fanciful, unrealistic…
   6. "disastrous"
      suggests horrific, life-threatening, widespread effects of existing laws
   7. "impact"
      suggests powerful, negative, destructive force of existing laws

Sentence structure:
   8. "Good grief"
      positioning at start of sentence establishes exasperated tone of diatribe to follow
   9. "…and often disastrous,"
      adds additional layer of criticism
  10. rhetorical question
      stylistic device inviting reader to share the writer's beliefs
  11. "not just … but"
      this construction allows the writer to

11. lines 38–43 (b) continued

      expand his argument into other areas, build his argument to a climax
  12. listing "on … on …on"
      repetitive structure suggests scale, variety of problems caused by current laws

Tone:
  13. scornful – "fond"
  14. satirical – "monstrous, Soviet-style diktats"
  15. exasperated, frustrated, angry, incredulous – "Good grief", "what on earth do they imagine"
  16. passionate, increasingly angry – "on employment … on economic growth?"

12. Possible answers

Ideas:
   1. writer brings argument back to shortage of housing – a key issue introduced in the opening paragraph and referred to throughout the passage
   2. writer focuses again on the selfishness, aggression, insularity, idealised views of the middle classes – themes discussed at various points throughout the passage.
   3. writer looks at those affected ("young and poor") by the middle classes' campaigns and the problems they have (lack of housing, inability to advance themselves, long distances to travel to work) – attempting to damn the middle classes' opposition.

Style:
   4. "And … on homelessness"
      link to or climax of argument from previous paragraph, returning argument to its primary concern
   5. "homelessness"
      somewhat sensationalised term, a deliberate (and misleading?) attempt by the writer to evoke our sympathy
   6. "Every time"
      wearisome inevitability of middle class campaigning
   7. "bunch"
      suggests a gang or a loose grouping lacking authority or credibility; derogatory term continues criticism of middle classes
   8. "fights off"
      criticism of middle classes' combative, aggressive stance
   9. " 'intrusion' "
      use of inverted commas reiterates misguided nature of middle class objections
  10. "cherished landscape"
      satirical tone, once again poking fun at the middle classes' idealised, possessive vision of the countryside
  11. "young and poor"
      attempt to tug at the readers' heartstrings and emphasise the cruelty of the middle classes' opposition

12. continued

12. "reasonable proximity", "somewhere to live"
the reasonable, understated goals of those seeking houses stand in contrast to the middle classes' unyielding, isolationist, unhelpful position

13. "pulling up drawbridge … castle"
extended metaphor again suggests the insular/selfish, feudal, old-fashioned, elitist, uncaring, NIMBYist nature of the middle classes.

Question on both Passages

13. The mark for this question should reflect the overall quality of the response and may not be directly related to the length of the response or to the number of points/reference made. A succinct sophisticated response should be worth more than a series of fairly trivial points and obvious references. "Ticking and adding up" is not appropriate (or fair) here.

For full marks there must be reference to both passages (although not necessarily a balanced treatment) and convincing evaluative comment. Where reference is made to one passage only, the maximum mark is 3.

The following points could be made, but all points which candidates propose will have to be judged on their merits:

Ideas - Passage 1
- surprise that there is such wide coverage of the countryside debate
- balance of ideas both past and present day
- awareness of the wide extent of claims put forward by conservationists
- strong feelings of those who feel the countryside is under threat
- writer's disapproval of action groups
- conservationists' view of our national identity is discredited
- concept of our national identity and the complexities involved
- history requires "continuous change"
- difficulties in establishing the "traditional British landscape"
- the landscape is determined by human influence not the environment

Style - Passage 1
- impersonal
- language used to highlight the strong feelings of conservationists: "so extensive …", "so fierce the passions …"
- repetition of "so"
- mocking tone
- word choice focusing on alleged dangers to the countryside: "mortal danger", "threatening", "killing", "overuse of machinery"
- tone of disapproval

13. continued

- word choice to discredit claims: "It might be thought", "widely assumed", "assumptions", "wildly overused term is seriously misleading"
- the short sentence to refute the claims: "This view is palpably nonsensical."
- imagery such as: "single thread", "bewildering array"
- balance of past/present
- impact of title/headline

Ideas - Passage 2
- the hypocrisy of the English middle classes regarding the countryside
- extreme nature of their view of the threat to the countryside
- the threat is much less serious than has been suggested
- some of the green belt around London should be used for housing
- the theory about green belts as "lungs" is a myth
- the flawed arguments of the "green-belt protectionists"
- green belts benefit property owners not those on inner city estates
- middle class homeowners react to any encroachment on their land and this makes it more difficult for the young and the poor to find suitable housing

Style - Passage 2
- personal involvement of the writer
- self-mocking tone regarding his own middle class position
- word choice to show extreme nature of the alleged threat to the countryside: "choked by concrete", "rapacious housebuilders"
- imagery in lines 11-19
- statistics in lines 20-24
- imagery in lines 25-32
- one-word sentence to dismiss claims made by conservationists: "Hogwash."
- conclusion: imagery of castle, drawbridge, …
- impact of title/headline

English Higher
Critical Essay
2008

1. Performance Criteria

While the Performance Criteria for 2008 are unchanged from previous years, the Categories and Descriptors in 2008 differ from those used in previous years.

Understanding

As appropriate to task, the response demonstrates secure understanding of key elements, central concerns and significant details of the *text(s).

Analysis

The response explains accurately and in detail ways in which relevant aspects of structure/style/ language contribute to meaning/effect/impact.

Evaluation

The response reveals clear engagement with the *text(s) or aspects of the text(s) and stated or implied evaluation of effectiveness, substantiated by detailed and relevant evidence from the *text(s).

Expression

Structure, style and language, including use of appropriate critical terminology, are deployed to communicate meaning clearly and develop a line of thought which is sustainedly relevant to purpose; spelling, grammar and punctuation are sufficiently accurate.

*The term "text" encompasses printed, audio or film/video text(s) which may be literary (fiction or non-fiction) or may relate to aspects of media or language.

2. Confirming Technical Accuracy

An essay which does not satisfy the requirement for "sufficient" technical accuracy cannot pass. If, however, technical accuracy is deemed "sufficient", then there are no penalties or deductions for such errors.

The definition of "sufficiently accurate" is the same as that given below for "consistently accurate", but with an allowance made for examination conditions, ie time pressure and no opportunity to redraft.

Consistently accurate (in line with Core Skills statement)

Few errors will be present. Paragraphs, sentences and punctuation are accurate and organised so that the writing can be clearly and readily understood. Spelling errors (particularly of high frequency words) are infrequent.

3. Assigning a Category and Mark

Each essay should then be assigned to the appropriate Category as outlined in the Broad Descriptors, supported by reference to the Detailed Descriptors.

(a) Broad Descriptors

Essays which **pass** (ie meet the minimum requirements of the Performance Criteria) should be assigned to one of four categories as follows:

Category	Mark(s)	Broad descriptor
I	25	Outstanding
II	21 **or** 23	Very sound
III	17 **or** 19	Comfortably achieves the Performance Criteria
IV	13 **or** 15	Just succeeds in achieving the Performance Criteria

Essays which **fail** to meet the minimum requirements of one or more than one Performance Criterion should be assigned to one of two categories as follows:

Category	Mark(s)	Broad descriptor
V	11 **or** 9	Fails to achieve one or more than one Performance Criterion and/or to achieve sufficient technical accuracy, or is simply too thin
VI*	7 **or** 5**	Serious shortcomings

In Categories II – VI, the choice of which mark to award should be determined by the level of certainty with which the response has been assigned to the Category.

*   Essays in this Category will be extremely rare. It should be used only in cases of significant misunderstanding of a text, extreme thinness, or serious weaknesses in expression and/or technical accuracy.

**   Marks below 5 could, in exceptional circumstances, be awarded – for example to a response which was of extreme brevity, perhaps just a few lines.

(b) Detailed descriptors

Category I (25 marks): A sophisticated response which, allowing for the pressures of examination conditions and the limited time available, is outstanding in nearly every respect. Knowledge and understanding of the text(s) are sound. The question is addressed fully and convincingly in such a way as to show insight

(*b*) **Detailed descriptors** continued

into the text(s) as a whole, and selection of evidence to support the argument is extensive and skilful. The essay is effectively structured as a genuine response to the question. As appropriate to the task and the text(s), the candidate demonstrates a sophisticated awareness of the literary and/or linguistic techniques being exploited. There is a committed evaluative stance with respect to the text(s) and the task, although this is not necessarily explicit. Expression is controlled and fluent.

Dealing with longer texts, the response ranges effectively over the whole text where appropriate, selects effectively, and while focusing on the demands of the question, never loses sight of the text as a whole; dealing with shorter texts, the response uses a text which clearly allows the requirements of the question to be met fully, avoids "blanket coverage" and mechanistic, unfocused "analysis", and shows a pleasing understanding of the text as a whole.

Category II (21 or 23 marks): A very sound response which, allowing for the pressures of examination conditions and the limited time available, is secure in most respects. Knowledge and understanding of the text(s) are sound. The question is addressed fully in such a way as to show some insight into the text(s) as a whole, and selection of evidence to support the argument is extensive. The essay is soundly structured as a genuine response to the question. As appropriate to the task and the text(s), the candidate demonstrates a sound awareness of the literary and/or linguistic techniques being exploited. There is a clear evaluative stance with respect to the text(s) and the task, although this is not necessarily explicit. Expression is controlled.

Dealing with longer texts, the response ranges over the whole text where appropriate, selects sensibly, and while focusing on the demands of the question, never loses sight of the text as a whole; dealing with shorter texts, the response uses a text which clearly allows the requirements of the question to be met, avoids "blanket coverage" and mechanistic, unfocused "analysis", and shows a sound understanding of the text as a whole.

Category III (17 or 19 marks): A response which, allowing for the pressures of examination conditions and the limited time available, is secure in a number of respects. Knowledge and understanding of the text(s) are on the whole sound. The question is addressed adequately in such a way as to show understanding of the text as a whole, and selection of evidence to support the argument is appropriate to the task. The essay is structured in such a way as to meet the requirements of the question. As appropriate to the task and the text(s), the candidate shows an awareness of the

literary and/or linguistic techniques being exploited. There is some evaluative stance with respect to the text(s) and the task, although this is not necessarily explicit. Expression is satisfactory.

Dealing with longer texts, the response makes some attempt to range over the whole text where appropriate, makes some selection of relevant evidence, and while focusing on the demands of the question, retains some sense of the text as a whole; dealing with shorter texts, the response uses a text which meets the requirements of the question, avoids excessive "blanket coverage" and mechanistic, unfocused "analysis", and shows an understanding of the text as a whole.

Category IV (13 or 15 marks): A response which, allowing for the pressures of examination conditions and the limited time available, just manages to meet the minimum standard to achieve the Performance Criteria. Knowledge and understanding of the text(s) are adequate. The question is addressed sufficiently in such a way as to show reasonable understanding of the text as a whole, and there is some evidence to support the argument. There is some evidence that the essay is structured in such a way as to meet the requirements of most of the question. As appropriate to the task and the text(s), the candidate shows some awareness of the literary and/or linguistic techniques being exploited. There is some evaluative stance with respect to the text(s) and the task, although this is not necessarily explicit. Expression is adequate.

Dealing with longer texts, the response retains some sense of the text as a whole; dealing with shorter texts, the response uses a text which meets the requirements of the question, avoids excessive use of mechanistic, unfocused "analysis", and shows some understanding of the text as a whole.

Category V (11 or 9 marks): A response will fall into this Category for a variety of reasons: it fails to achieve sufficient technical accuracy; or knowledge and understanding of the text are not deployed as a response relevant to the task; or any analysis attempted is undiscriminating and/or unfocused; or the answer is simply too thin.

Pocket answer section for SQA Higher English 2004–2008

© 2008 Scottish Qualifications Authority/Leckie & Leckie, All Rights Reserved
Published by Leckie & Leckie Ltd, 3rd Floor, 4 Queen Street, Edinburgh EH2 1JE
tel: 0131 220 6831, fax: 0131 225 9987, enquiries@leckieandleckie.co.uk, www.leckieandleckie.co.uk

English Higher
Close Reading 2004

Note that in 'Analysis' questions – i.e. 2(b), 4(a), 4(b)(ii), 5(b), 6, 9, 10(a), 10(c)(ii), 12 – marks are awarded solely for the quality of comment; no marks are given for simply picking out a word or an image, or for identifying a tone or a feature of sentence structure.

1. 1 (unnecessarily) fearful, worried, concerned, (over) anxious
2 suspicious of everyone / everything
3 always fearing the worst
4 unable to leave the children to their own devices
1 mark will also be given for appropriate reference to parents' questions, worries, concerns.

2. (a) The story shows that:
1 an apparently serious incident had an innocent explanation
2 people are too ready to rush to judgement
3 rushing to judgement is wrong
4 teacher / social workers / authorities misinterpreted the situation
5 teacher / social workers / authorities were made to look foolish
6 it is a further example of "paranoia"
7 it is a feature of our age
8 other appropriate answer

(b) *Teacher:*
1 "zealous" (line 18)
suggests over-enthusiastic, fanatical, driven by personal agenda, ...
2 "ever alert" (line 19)
slightly mocking, suggesting keenness to find fault, ...
3 "omnipresence" (line 19)
exaggeration
4 "one look" (line 20)
emphasises precipitate action
5 "hissed" (line 22)
suggests vicious, spiteful, animal-like, ...
6 "clearly" (line 22)
shows certainty, lack of any doubt, ...

Social Workers:
7 "rushed" (line 23)
speed, lack of deliberation, ...
8 "quiz" (line 24)
suggestion of intrusive questioning, ...

Either:
9 "once upon a time" (line 9)
suggests living in fantasy / fairy-tale world

3. Marks will be awarded for:
1. a clear understanding of "A fairy tale's power lies in its ability to express authentic fears" –

3. continued
e.g. the impact of such a story comes from the way it can articulate real worries
and / or
2. a clear understanding of: "...this one reveals the paranoia that now prevails ..." – e.g. such a story exposes the irrational fears which are widespread
and / or
3. a clear understanding of "urban myth" as an articulation of real fears.

4. (a) Possible answers include:
Word choice:
1 "permanently ... worse still... every ... immediately ... perpetual ... everyone" concentration of intensifying words

2 "threat ... bad ... suspicion" connotations of danger, evil

Sentence structure:
3 repetition of "we" / "we live"
rhetorical / emotional device; sense of inclusiveness; demonstrates extent of problem

4 positioning of "Collectively"
to intensify universality

5 the two sentences from "Collectively ..." to "... us." contain a number of relevant features (e.g. climax, balancing round semi-colon, ...) and appropriate comment could be made on any of these

Sound:
6 alliteration of "Collectively" and "convinced" contains a hint of (self-)mockery

Imagery:
7 "absurd heights"
it will not be easy to make appropriate comment since this is in the question, but it might be possible

(b) (i) contempt, mockery, disapproval, anger, ...

(ii) Possible answers include:
1 "paranoia" (line 46)
implies their behaviour is irrational, ...
2 "artful" (line 46)
implies they're self-serving, sly, ...
3 "something terrible" (line 47)
ironic tone – examples are fairly innocuous
4 inverted commas at "dangerous" (line 49)
to point up falseness, exaggeration, implication they're not dangerous at all
5 "sirens / blue lights"(lines 49–50)
over-reaction, trivializing as a spectacle, assumption of guilt

English Higher
Close Reading
2004 (cont.)

4. (b) (ii) continued

6   "industry" (line 52)
      suggests organized nature, large scale,
      empire-building, profit-making

7   "(bout of) self-importance" (line 53)
      accuses them of taking themselves too
      seriously

8   "Mee-maw, mee-maw." (line 54)
      imitation of the sound suggests they are
      childish, ...

9   "Clear the area, please." (line 54)
      paints them as authoritarian,
      overbearing, pushy...

10   "expert" (line 55)
      perhaps people who call themselves
      "experts" are not to be trusted

11   "doom-mongers" (line 55)
      as if tragedy / injury is their living, they
      thrive on it, ...

5. (a) A good gloss of "devoid of freedom, decision-making, and the opportunity to take their own risks" will gain marks.
Alternatively, a more general summary of the paragraph along the lines of "They are being denied experiences from the 'real' world" will also gain marks.
Excessive use of the concrete (e.g. references to helmets, sledging, cycling, trees, etc) rather than the abstract will constitute a weakness.

(b) For full marks an answer must make clear the root and the implication of the image (that the unnatural, restricted, unhealthy, cruel environment in which battery hens are raised is being compared with the way children today are being denied real, healthy, risky experiences) and make some evaluative comment.

6. (a) (i) anger, contempt, frustration, ...
     get: tired, bored, weary, ...

   (ii) Possible answers:
1   repetitive structure of "I'm fed up ... I am weary ... I am sick ..."
     drives home the point forcefully
2   word choice in "fed up ... weary ... sick"
     exaggerated connotations of illness, depression, ...
3   word choice in "scaremongers"/"lurk"
     connotation of threat
4   use of intensifiers: "never ... everywhere ... never"
     emphatic, strong personal commitment
5   balancing of "on the one hand ... at the same time"
     points up the contradictory, illogical attitude

6 .(b) Possible answers:
Sentence structure:
1 positioning of "Everywhere" (line 80)
   emphatic exaggeration
2 the parenthesis about the media (line 81)
   sneering tone
3 the string of sentences beginning "Don't ..." (lines 83-92)
   emphasises their negative, authoritarian attitude
4 the repeated structure of command followed by reason (line 83-91)
   as above, or emphasises the weak justifications (in writer's eyes)
5 "And on and on it goes." (line 92)
   deliberately glib, repetitive, ...

Tone:
6 "ably abetted" (line 81)
   sarcastic, sneering
7 "hard at work" (lines 81-82)
   ironic – she doesn't value their work at all
8 "brain themselves" (lines 87-88)
   use of colloquialism for humour
9 "sizzle their brains" (lines 90-91)
   use of exaggeration, colloquialism for humour
10 "And on and on it goes" (line 92)
   (mock) weariness, distaste, ...

Word choice:
11 "army" (line 80)
   large numbers, organised, overwhelming, threatening, ...
12 "abetted" (line 81)
   suggests underhand activity, criminality, ...

7. Any two of the following could be included in a good answer:
1   they are frightened of accusation (from parents and / or children)
2   they are unable to give their best
3   the atmosphere is not conducive to helping young people

8. In a good answer candidates will show a clear grasp of the key idea that despite the worries of some (paranoid) parents, the trip was a success. They should also show, with appropriate reference, how effectively (or not) this supports the thrust of her argument in the article thus far.
Note that the question refers to ideas, not style or language, although it is possible that these may be used appropriately to support candidates' comments on the anecdote.

9. Possible answers:
Word choice / imagery:
1   "pit"
     suggestion of low, dark, murky, infernal, ...
2   "exaggerated"
     suggestion of illogical, unfounded, ...
3   "irrational"
     suggestion of mental weakness, ...
4   "spiral"
     suggestion of being out of control, ...

9. continued

5 "overwhelmingly"
suggestion of something devastating, crushing, ...

6 "utterly"
very emphatic, hint of despair, ...

7 "catastrophic"
as big a disaster as can be imagined, ...

Sentence structure:

8 "But so deep are we ..."
inversion for rhetorical effect, emphasis on "deep"

9 balance of "might go wrong ... *will* go wrong"
rhetorical (also use of italics just in case the point is missed)

10 the brevity of "It is a dangerous spiral" and / or "It is utterly catastrophic"
emphatic

11 the repetition of "It is ..."
preachy, hectoring, ...

12 the listing of "... death, disease, accident, or injury ..."
to emphasise the range of threats nowadays reduced

13 the intrusive parenthesis in "For.. dangerous" delaying the main clause
dramatic, rhetorical, ...

14 brevity of "It is utterly catastrophic."
emphatic conclusion

Tone:

15 anger, despair, moral superiority, established by almost any of the above

10. (*a*) A good answer should include the straightforward explanation that a pendulum swings from one extreme / side to the other, as have views on how to care for children.

(*b*) Answers should include the meaning of the word "cosseting": e.g. pamper, over-protect, spoil, ...
Reference should also be made to or explanation of context, e.g.

1 "excessively protective"
2 "always worrying (about germs)"
3 "obsession with our child's safety"
4 "playing areas covered with rubber"
5 "*Paranoid Parenting*"

(*c*) (i) Answers can include any of the following:

1 they are not dangerous enough
2 they shouldn't be protected (with rubber)
3 they are too safe

(ii) One mark for defining attitude, e.g. it is wrong, stupid, dangerous, ...
One mark for observing / illustrating that the (humorous) exaggeration makes the tone sarcastic, mocking, ...

11. Answers should refer to both sides of the argument:
Furedi wishes a reduction in car journeys to school or thinks that it is bad for children to be driven to school.
UNICEF figures show that this actually makes them safer.

12. A good answer will pick up on the mocking, derisory attitude developed through the wild exaggeration or tongue-in-cheek tone. This should be supported with appropriate (ideally succinct) references.

13. The following two points would constitute an ideal answer:

1 parents who look after or are concerned for their children aren't doing anything wrong
2 those who criticise parents for being protective are adding to parents' worries

14. Note that the question is on "ideas", not language or style. While it will not be wholly inappropriate for candidates to refer to, for example, Reid's rhetoric and / or Bennett's humour, the thrust of the answer must address the writers' ideas about Furedi and his beliefs.
A good answer will have a clear and intelligent understanding of both passages, including evaluative comments that are thoughtful and convincing.

English Higher
Critical Essay
2004

Marking principles for Critical Essay are as follows

- Each essay should first be read to establish whether the essay achieves success in **all** the Performance Criteria for Grade C, including relevance and the standards for technical accuracy outlined in Note 1 below.

- If minimum standards are not achieved in any **one** or more of the Performance Criteria, the maximum mark which can be awarded is 11.

- If minimum standards have been achieved, then the supplementary marking grids will allow you to place the work on a scale of marks out of 25.

- The Category awarded and the mark should be placed at the end of the essay.

Notes

1. "Sufficiently accurate" can best be defined in terms of a definition of "consistently accurate".

    Consistently accurate

    Few errors will be present. The candidate may use complex language. Sentences may be internally complex in terms of main and subordinate clauses. Paragraphs, sentences and punctuation are organised so that linkage and expression allow clear understanding of the writing. Spelling errors (particularly of high frequency words) should be infrequent

    Sufficiently accurate

    As above but with an allowance made for speed and the lack of opportunity to redraft.

2. Using the Category descriptions

    Categories are not grades. Although derived from performance criteria for Grade C and the indicators of excellence for Grade A, the four categories are designed primarily to assist with placing each candidate response at an appropriate point on a continuum of achievement. Assumptions about final grades or association of final grades with particular categories should not be allowed to influence objective assessment.

    Once an essay has been deemed to pass the basic criteria, it does not have to meet all the suggestions for Category II (for example) to fall into that Category. More typically there will be a spectrum of strengths and weaknesses which span categories. Assessment at this stage is holistic.

All critical essay questions require candidates to select from their knowledge of a text in order to shape a response to a specific question. Thus, obviously "prepared" answers which entirely fail to focus on the question cannot pass. Similarly, blanket coverage (especially of a poem) which merely touches on the question is very unlikely to do well.

Grade C
Performance Criteria

(a) *Understanding*
As appropriate to task, the response demonstrates secure understanding of key elements, central concerns and significant details of the text(s).

(b) *Analysis*
The response explains accurately and in detail ways in which relevant aspects of structure/style/language contribute to meaning/effect/impact.

(c) *Evaluation*
The response reveals clear engagement with the text(s) or aspects of the text(s) and stated or implied evaluation of effectiveness, substantiated with detailed and relevant evidence from the text(s).

(d) *Expression*
Structure, style and language, including appropriate critical terminology, are deployed to communicate meaning clearly and develop a line of thought which is consistently relevant to purpose; spelling, grammar and punctuation are sufficiently accurate.

Critical Essay (Higher)—Supplementary Advice

This advice, which is supplementary to the Performance Criteria, is designed to assist with the placing of scripts within the full range of marks. However, the Performance Criteria as published give the primary definitions. The mark range for each Category is identified.

IV 8–11	III 12–15	II 16–19	I 20–25
An essay which falls into this category may do so for a variety of reasons.	**Understanding** • Knowledge of the text(s), and a secure understanding of the central concerns will be used.	**Understanding** • Knowledge and understanding of the central concerns of the text(s) will be clearly demonstrated.	**Understanding** • Thorough knowledge and insight into the central concerns of the text(s) will be demonstrated at this level.
It could be • that it fails to achieve consistent technical accuracy. • or that any knowledge and understanding of the text(s) is not deployed as a response relevant to the task. • or that analysis and evaluation attempted are unconvincing. • or that the answer is simply too thin.	• to provide an answer relevant to the task. • Detailed reference to the text(s) to support the candidate's argument will be made.	• and deployed sensibly to form a sound developed answer which is relevant to the task. • Detailed reference to the text(s) will be used appropriately as evidence for the candidate's argument.	• and there will be a relevant, well-structured response to the demands of the task. • Extensive and skilful reference to the text(s) will be used appropriately as evidence for the argument.
	Analysis • There will be an accurate explanation of the contribution of literary/ linguistic techniques to the impact of the text.	**Analysis** • There will be analysis of literary/ linguistic techniques and how they affect the impact of the text(s).	**Analysis** • There will be a convincing evaluative analysis of the writer's literary and linguistic techniques.
	Evaluation • There will be a positive engagement with the text(s) which will state or imply an evaluation of its effectiveness.	**Evaluation** • There will be a positive engagement with the text(s) (which may be implicit) leading to a considered evaluative stance with respect to the text(s).	**Evaluation** • There will be an appreciative response allied to a committed stance with respect to the text(s) which may be implicit.
	Expression • Language will communicate the argument clearly, and there will be appropriate critical terminology deployed. Spelling, grammar and punctuation will be sufficiently accurate.	**Expression** • Language will be used confidently and the deployment of critical terminology will add to the strength of the candidate's argument.	**Expression** • The language used will be controlled and fluent, making accurate and appropriate use of critical terminology in pursuit of a skilful analysis.
		At this level there should be no doubt that the question has been answered out of a sound knowledge and understanding of the text(s).	An answer of this standard will give the impression that it is drawing skilfully on an extensive knowledge of the text(s) to focus on the demands of the question.

English Higher
Close Reading
2005

1. (a) *Any two of*
    1 It wiped out/destroyed …
    2 … half of the existing life-forms …
    3 … including dinosaurs
Alternatively, an understanding of the implication of "significant breakthrough" causing change to scientific thinking.

  (b) *Any one of*
    1 They used information provided by fossils.
    2 They counted the objects in space surrounding the earth.
    3 They employed clever methods of detection.

2. (a)
    1 gloss on "driving force" (1 mark) – e.g. cause, factor, impetus, agent of change
    2 gloss on "evolutionary change" (1 mark) – e.g. development, the way the species has evolved

  (b) *Any two of*
    1 Comets and other fragments combined to create the earth.
    2 Comets contained water which allowed life to develop.
    3 Comets brought the organic elements which are necessary for life.
    4 Comets and change often coincided.
    5 Collisions sometimes caused almost complete extinction of species/life.
    6 After collisions new forms of life emerged.

  (c) Possible Answers:
    Structure:
    1 openings of sentences: reference to some of "Originally/After that …"
    convey a sequence through time of effects caused on the planet by comet impact
    2 repetition of simple sentence structure (of the first three sentences)
    contributes to the ongoing, repetitive, inevitable nature of the effects of comets on creation
    3 structure of last two sentences (e.g. placing of "all life" and "wiped out")
    could be seen as climactic, dramatically emphasising point
    Word choice:
    4 "smashed"/"slammed"
    connotations of the force/impact/violence with which these objects hit earth
    5 "violence"
    emphasises force, suggestion of aggression
    6 "precipitated"
    brought matters to an extreme point, connotations of lack of control
    7 "extinction"
    extremity of the danger to life
    8 "catastrophe"
    idea of total, extreme devastation

2. (c) (continued)
    9 "wiped out" total nature of disaster/ blanket disappearance
    Imagery:
    10 "punctuate the story" just as punctuation marks show divisions in a sentence or paragraph, the impacts act as landmarks, divisions in the history/narrative of the earth's evolution
    11 "aftermath" just as there is debris left after harvesting, there were the later (bad) consequences of impacts
    12 "wiped out" just as a blackboard etc can be wiped clean of any marks or meaning, the damage caused by impacts was total

3. (a) *Any two of*
    1 The idea that "lucky" or "the essentially random nature of impacts" is incompatible with the logical/purposeful progression implied by the theory of the survival of the fittest.
    2 Collisions have changed the course of evolution more than the innate ability of the strong of a species to survive.
    3 The effort put into surviving in a particular environment is wasted when that environment suddenly changes.

  (b) Possible answers include:
    1 use of "lucky"
    not usual scientific terminology, suggests a more flippant approach
    2 use of "dust settled"
    literal/metaphorical ambiguity could be seen as humorous
    3 "being thumped (on the head)"
    unscientific terminology creates a humorous picture
    4 "thumped" and "conducive" (or any similar combination)
    juxtaposition of colloquial and formal gives rise to humour
    5 "not conducive to a long and happy existence"
    ironic, understated, deliberately clichéd, contrast with "thumped"
    6 use of italics/inverted commas to suggest method of vocal delivery
    creates comic effect and emphasis

4. Possible answers include:
  1 The universe/our world is essentially an indifferent/hostile place for humans as well as other species.
  2 Our survival is a matter of luck.
  3 We are just as likely to become extinct as other species have (because we have no defence against these enormously powerful, random events).
  4 We have no special protection from the elemental forces of the universe.

5. *Any two of*

   1 The mention of "three questions" followed by a colon leads to expectation that three questions (about the possibility/implications of comet impact) will appear after the colon.

   2 The use of two semi-colons to separate the three questions helps us to isolate each of the questions (about the possibility/implications of comet impact).

   3 The use of the question mark at the end of the sentence helps to remind us of the fact that we are dealing with a series of questions (about the possibility/implications of comet impact).

6. The answer should refer to "religious significance" or "long-held beliefs" or "legendary" or "ancient beliefs, legends, sagas and myths" and show recognition of its/their non-scientific nature.

7. Main idea: by comparison with other threats, comet impact is much more serious.
   Final sentence intensifies/makes clear the main idea by any of:

   1 reinforcing/expanding the idea of widespread devastation

   2 using understatement, irony, scientist's idea of humour

   3 making an unexpected addition, afterthought

   4 using a relatively short sentence

   5 by starting the sentence, unusually, with "And"

   6 any other acceptable answer

8. Some indication that the candidate understands the term "irony".
   The key idea is that we have become so advanced in our knowledge of the universe, we are able to see that our destruction is likely.
   It might be argued that there is irony in the idea that the threat of comet impact was in fact not a "threat" to the human race because it was a contributor to our emergence as a species, ie something positive.

9. (*a*) 1 Do nothing (and just hope that no comet hits us too hard).

   2 Take preventative action (against the comets/asteroids so that they don't hit the earth).

   (*b*) Possible comments:

   1 "heated"
   just as objects, liquids etc when heated are more volatile, full of movement etc, the debate has become voluble, possibly loud, animated, …

   2 "ferment"
   just as the process of brewing causes movement, effervescence, explosions etc, the debate has become lively, loud, possibly "dangerous", …

   3 "brewing"
   just as the process of brewing causes movement, effervescence, heady liquids etc, the debate is developing, growing voluble, loud, …

9. (*b*) (continued)

   4 "symptom"
   just as a symptom is the outward sign of an underlying disease the debate is the outward sign of the underlying vigorous controversy

   (*c*) Possible approaches:

   1 Take action; because, while recognising that there are other, more probable, dangers to our lives, he points out that comet/asteroid impact could kill everyone.

   2 Take action; because saying "…but that is not the point" implies something else is (recognising the extent of the devastation comet/asteroid impact would create) and must be addressed.

   3 Take action; because the acknowledgement that there are other dangers is dismissed with a curt: "…but that is not the point".

   4 Take action; deliberate contrast between "cost us our lives" and "cost all of us our lives" (with italicisation to underline the difference) shows one threat is more serious than the other and should, by implication, be addressed more seriously.

   5 Do nothing; it is a decision that cannot be made now; we need to learn more first; "great deal more" implies we know very little or don't know enough at the moment.

   6 Do nothing; he merely poses a question (and refers to "ask" and "question") and uses conditional and future ideas ("risk", "future", "may", "will") – not indicative of strong feeling for doing something now.

   7 His stance is ambiguous; a combination of any of the above.

10. Possible features/techniques/comments:

   1 use of "It" to open the article
   mysterious; mystery is not solved until paragraph two

   2 word choice:
   "destroy … plunge … giant … racing … unleash … crashing … hurtling … direct hit … huge … billions … blocking out … perish … starve …devastating"
   The vocabulary chosen conveys violence or speed or power or size or disastrous effects of an asteroid striking Earth.

   3 imagery (e.g. "unleash")
   appropriate deconstruction and comment

   4 illustrative detail
   used to convey: size (Belgium is an entire country);
   time (the Dark Ages suggests the severity of the consequences); speed/power (comparison to the Hiroshima explosion suggests the scale of the potential disaster)

   5 use of climax and anti-climax
   tension built up to the final sentence in both paragraphs; use of anti-climax to a lesser extent at the end of paragraph one and much more obviously at the end of paragraph two where the odds are quoted (1 in 909,000).

   6 use of statistics/dates
   to convey sheer scale and/or precision

English Higher
Close Reading
2005 (cont.)

11. Possible answers:
    Confidence:
    1 "Astrophysics expert", "Dr", "University"
       suggest academic ability and success
    2 "advises"
       recognition in his field
    3 "accuracy", "rule out", "will"
       suggest knowledge and precision
    Lack of confidence:
    4 "NEO (Near Earth Objects)"
       vagueness of title does not inspire
    5 "optimistic"
       idea of being hopeful, not necessarily supported
       by facts
    6 "In all probability"
       not complete certainty

12. *Meaning:* e.g. total destruction; an event of such
    decisiveness and on such a scale that survival is
    most unlikely...
    Context: Any one of
    1 "wipe out most of the human race"
    2 "the end of the world is nigh"
    3 the force of final short sentence "But the end is
       nigh."
    4 "face" suggests an ordeal and may gain some
       credit

13. Possible answers
    Paragraphs 1-4 (lines1-42):
    dramatic, hysterical, sensational, emotive ...
    supported by reference to or comment on the use
    of opinions, sensationalism, etc
    Paragraph 5 (lines 43-53):
    factual, scientific, historical ...
    supported by reference to background detail such
    as research findings or past events, etc

14. Possible answers:
    Sentence structure:
    1 step by step account
    2 sentences become shorter
    3 builds up to a very short final sentence
    4 goes from general to the specific
    5 repetition of "dark" (with the reinforcing initial
       "And")
    6 accumulative negatives – "no power, no
       communications, no infrastructure."
    7 repetition of "back"
    Verb tense:
    8 (future tense changes to) present tense
       immediacy of the sudden impact, lack of time
       to take evasive action ...
    Word choice:
    9 "injected" suggestion of force, alien material
    10 "cold", "dark"
       bleakness
    11 "die out", "lose"
       sense of loss, extinction, mortality, ...
    12 (repetition of) "no"
       negative impact

15. *Any one of*
    1 Bookmakers are accepting money knowing there
       will be no payout.
    2 Winners will not be alive to claim their
       winnings.
    3 Anyone making money so easily would be
       happy.

16. Note that the question is on "ideas and style".
    The mark for this question will reflect the overall
    quality of the response and may not be directly
    related to the length of the response or to the
    number of points/references made. A succinct,
    sophisticated response is worth more than a series
    of fairly trivial points and obvious references.
    For full marks there must be reference to both
    elements (ie ideas and style) and to both passages
    (although not necessarily a balanced treatment)
    and convincing evaluative comment.
    Possible points:
    Ideas:
    • theoretical/philosophical ideas more important
       in Passage 1
    • practical problems mainly in Passage 2
    Style:
    • language more sensational/immediate in
       Passage 2
    • more human interest in Passage 2
    • use of illustration to explain in Passage 1
    • contrast in tone at end of passages

English Higher
Critical Essay
2005

Please refer to the answer guidelines given for the Critical Essay in English Higher 2004.

English Higher
Close Reading
2006

1. (a) A brief reference to the change from concern about (the effects of) too little food to concern about (the effects of) too much

   (b) *Possible answers include*:
   1. Parallelism/balanced construction
   2. Series of contrasts ("when/now" ... "fat/thin" ... "feed the hungry/obesity")
   3. Repetition of "rich...poor...right-thinking"
   4. Two compound sentences with co-ordinate clauses in which the attributes are reversed

2. *Any two of the following*:
   1. acceptable gloss on "has designed mankind"
   2. humans have the ability to survive shortages by storing reserves
   3. in a period of continuous prosperity people become increasingly bigger

3. (a) *Either of the following*:
   1. they have been proved wrong
   2. (although the population of the world has risen) the number of people who are hungry has fallen.

   (b) "cause for celebration"
   There is now, according to the writer, sufficient food for mankind.
   "mostly"
   The drawback is that we now have another problem.

   (c) *Possible answers include*:
   1. "won ... battle"
   idea of struggle, succeeding in a difficult situation
   2. "offspring"
   idea of product, source ... importance of survival of the genetic line
   3. "silver lining"
   idea of shining/bright side, redeeming aspect of an otherwise unpleasant situation
   4. "cloud"
   dull or dark spot, sense of threat
   5. "plague"
   idea of deadly epidemic, potential devastation caused by problem
   6. "host"
   idea of large number, threat, army (+ possible link to "won ... battle").

4. *Possible answers include*:
   Sentence structure:
   1. generic statement/assertion (lines 35–37) appears to brook no argument
   2. single dash
   used to explain/exemplify the opening statement by introducing the main risk
   3. semi-colons
   used to separate items in a list which emphasises the serious/life-threatening consequences of obesity

English Higher
Close Reading
2006 (cont.)

4. (continued)

    4.   listing
        emphasises the number and/or cumulative effect of health-related problems

    5.   second sentence
        provides a summation of the dire effects of obesity

Word choice:

    6.   "no doubt"
        emphatic

    7.   "biggest"
        use of superlative

    8.   "main cause"
        idea of strength/power

    9.   "kills"
        idea of deadly threat

    10. "principal risk factor"
        idea of statistical approach to danger

    11. "heavily implicated"
        idea of blame

    12. "labelled"
        idea of superficiality, pejorative tag

    13. "epidemic"
        idea of a disease out of control

    14. "fearful consequences"
        idea of a frightening, menacing future

    15. "thick and fast"
        idea that the extent/volume/speed of the reaction is almost out of control

Tone:

    16. any acceptable suggestion, e.g. relentlessly serious, slightly melodramatic, possibly ironic... – supported by appropriate reference and explanation

5. Cause for hope
    Any one of the following:
    1.   gloss on "public health warnings" and "media pressure"
    2.   reduction in smoking
    3.   increase in sale of health foods
    4.   (slight) reduction in weight of Americans
    Cause for concern
    Either of the following:
    5.   it will require a lengthy period of time for people to shed so much excess weight
    6.   meanwhile, there is an increase in weight throughout the more prosperous parts of the world.

6. (*a*) In the past: to assure quality of food/make food safer/guarantee regular availability of food.
        Now: gloss on "changing their behaviour", eg to transform eating habits.

6. (*b*) "bad reason" (lines 80–98)
        The crux of the paragraph is in lines 89–98 ("But ..."). Include a clear explanation of the writer's objections in terms of the "nanny state", intrusion into personal freedom, discouragement of personal responsibility, etc.
        "first good reason" (lines 99–120)
        The crux of the paragraph is the government's role in the protection of children, who are vulnerable/at risk for biological and/or social and/or commercial reasons.
        "second good reason" (lines 121–133)
        The crux is in the financial argument about the "unfairness"/imbalance in terms of contributions to and burdens upon the NHS.

7. *Possible answers include*:
    Sentence structure:
    1.   bluntness of opening "It might"
    2.   parenthesis for "(or might not)" – throwaway remark
    3.   use of "But" at start of sentence – clear indication of contradiction to come
    4.   repetition of "legitimate interest" – rhetorical device to squash his earlier case
    5.   delayed "let them" at end of paragraph – dismissive
    Word choice:
    6.   formality of word choice ("constitute ... intrusion on liberty ... gain in equity and efficiency ... legitimate interest") – bombastic, legalistic overtones.
    7.   informality of word choice ("stick its nose ... grossness ... early grave") – blunt, direct
    Tone:
    8.   contemptuous - informality/vulgarity of "stick its nose ... grossness ... early grave"
    9.   elevated, rather hectoring – "constitute ... intrusion on liberty ... private sphere"
    Contrast:
    10. contrast in register and/or tone (see 6, 7, 8 and 9 above)
    Sound:
    11. alliteration in "grossness ... grave" – harsh, contemptuous

8. (*a*) Show an understanding of "well-meaning" and of "misguided" and imply the contradiction, eg: The school thought it was healthy to ban sweets, but they caused the sweets to become even more attractive in the pupils' eyes.

    (*b*) The attitude – one of defiance/rebellion/anti-authoritarianism – should be implied.
        Possible answers include:
        1. "(away from the) teachers' eyes"
           suggests avoidance of authority of the all-seeing classroom eye
        2. "traded"
           suggests an illicit, appealing bargaining

8. (*b*) 3. "(marks of) rebellion"
exaggerates the significance of the swapping, but leaves the idea of the anti-authoritarian behaviour

4. "(statements of) independence"
suggests the dawning awakening of action not sanctioned by authority

5. "suspected"/"rather they didn't"
suggests a confused delight in thwarting the wishes of adults

6. "ever so much more"
suggests the excessive importance placed on a few relatively unimportant sweets

7. "enticing"
suggests the illicit, forbidden fruit idea

8. "not just food but"
suggests that the sweets had become an anti-authoritarian symbol

9. "food plus attitude"
suggests the sweets acquired a significance in the adoption of a stance against authority which soared beyond their importance as sweets.

9. Motivation: money-making/financial advantage/economic growth.
Illustrated by:
Those who are likely to make money (e.g. slimming clubs, chemists, doctors, campaigning organisations) will make it sound like an illness so they can be paid to treat it.

10. *Possible answers include*:
1. "So..."
introduces a sentence which sums up the argument so far

2. the use of short sentences
gives each idea an importance of its own for us to digest and recognise; sense of stating simple indisputable fact

3. "fitness, not fat, ..."
the balance/contrast is highlighted by the separation by commas or by the alliteration

4. "You..."
direct address, inclusive lead-in to final point

5. the list in the last sentence
short, punchy, climactic; helps us to reach an easily understood conclusion

11. (*a*) *Possible answers include*:
Word choice/imagery:
1. "danger"
suggestion of threat

2. "mimic"
suggestion of unthinking acceptance

3. "dogma"
suggestion of irrational, unbending, obstructive views

4. "demonisation"
suggestion of threat from evil forces, a satanic process

5. "hysteria"
suggestion of irrational fears being exploited

11. (*a*) (continued)
Sentence structure:
6. "who profits and who hurts"
summing up, simplifying the argument, bringing it to a head and emphasising "hurts"

7. climax (after pause created by semicolon)
as for point 6

Tone:
8. any sensible suggestion such as scathing, critical, dogmatic, hectoring ... – supported by appropriate reference and explanation.

(*b*) Answers should show a clear understanding that the "corrective" is for us to be aware of the distorting effects of the alteration to the BMI – that it makes the numbers of obese people seem greater or that it has caused quite ordinary-sized people to be classed as obese/overweight.

12. *Possible answers include*:
Sentence structure:
1. Short sentence - "There is a lot to be done" sets up an unmistakable agenda which acts as the topic for the rest of the paragraph

2. Repetition of "We need"
harps on the necessity for doing something, sets up a badgering, hectoring tone

3. Use of "And" to begin the final sentence by separating the final point into a distinct sentence we focus on who should be blamed for this confusion – the commercial interests

4. Climactic nature of the paragraph repetition of "We need" followed by the final "And we need" sets up a climax which is also emphasised by the use of short sentences followed by longer ones making us focus on the exploitative industries.

Word choice:
5. "emotional lives"
the idea that we are too captive to our feelings

6. "transform"
the change needs to be more than minor – transformation suggests a profound and far-reaching change

7. "culture (of thinness)"
suggests that thinness as an ideal has become deeply embedded in the way of life and assumptions of society

8. "deeply (confused)"
the problems are profound and will need a huge effort to eradicate them

9. "cynically" (promoted)
our anxieties are being exploited for gain

10. "selling (us)"
suggests that there needs to be a salesman who will exaggerate the problems associated with the idea of obesity

11. "(obesity) epidemic"
suggests that the situation is out of control like an infectious disease which cannot be stopped

Tone:
12. any sensible suggestion such as hectoring, pleading, impatient ... – supported by appropriate reference and explanation, probably to one or more of 1-11 above

English Higher
Close Reading
2006 (cont.)

13. (*a*) Passage 1: obesity is the greatest danger, a
major danger, a serious problem …

Passage 2: obesity is not such a big problem as
is being suggested and/or people are
making money from exaggerating
the problem

NB: The difference may be established
implicitly, e.g. "Passage 2 thinks obesity is not a
big problem".

(*b*) Note that the question asks for concentration on
style of writing, although there is reference to
the "opening stages of an argument". Implicit
understanding of each writer's point of view
will certainly be a feature of good answers. A
succinct, sophisticated response is worth more
than a series of fairly trivial points and obvious
references.

For full marks, there must be reference to both
passages (although not necessarily a balanced
treatment) and convincing evaluative comment.

Possible points:

Passage 1:

- the wordplay in paragraph 1, use of
repetition, parallelism
- the short sentence to highlight main cause:
evolution
- word choice such as "expanding bellies",
"fearful consequences" …
- the use of statistics/selection of dramatic,
serious illnesses
- imagery such as "battle", "plague" …
- wordplay in "every silver lining has a cloud"
…
- climactic nature of sentence structure (lines
35-45)

Passage 2:

- the nature of the introductory
anecdote/human interest story
- word choice such as "food plus attitude",
"swamping", "trumpet", "serious money" …
- exaggeration such as "endless", "destabilise",
"swamping", "millions" …
- language of business/money such as
"commercial", "industry", "market", "profit"
…
- sentence structure of lines 45-51

**English Higher
Close Reading
2006 (cont.)**

English Higher
Critical Essay 2006

All critical essay questions require candidates to select from their knowledge of a text in order to shape a response to a specific question. Thus, obviously "prepared" answers which entirely fail to focus on the question cannot pass. Similarly, blanket coverage (especially of a poem) which merely touches on the question is very unlikely to do well.

Marking principles for Critical Essay are as follows

- Each essay should first be read to establish whether the essay achieves success in **all** the Performance Criteria, including relevance and the standards for technical accuracy outlined in Note 2 below.

- If minimum standards are not achieved in any **one** or more of the Performance Criteria, the maximum mark which can be awarded is 11.

- If minimum standards have been achieved, then the supplementary marking grids will allow you to place the work on a scale of marks out of 25.

Notes

1. Using the Category descriptions

    Categories are not grades. Although derived from performance criteria for Grade C and the indicators of excellence for Grade A, the four categories are designed primarily to assist with placing each candidate response at an appropriate point on a continuum of achievement. Assumptions about final grades or association of final grades with particular categories should not be allowed to influence objective assessment.

    Once an essay has been deemed to pass the basic criteria, it does not have to meet all the suggestions for Category II (for example) to fall into that Category. More typically there will be a spectrum of strengths and weaknesses which span categories. Assessment at this stage is holistic.

2. "Sufficiently accurate" can best be defined in terms of a definition of "consistently accurate".

    Consistently accurate

    Few errors will be present. The candidate may use complex language. Sentences may be internally complex in terms of main and subordinate clauses. Paragraphs, sentences and punctuation are organised so that linkage and expression allow clear understanding of the writing. Spelling errors (particularly of high frequency words) should be infrequent

    Sufficiently accurate

    As above but with an allowance made for speed and the lack of opportunity to redraft.

Performance Criteria

(a) *Understanding*
    As appropriate to task, the response demonstrates secure understanding of key elements, central concerns and significant details of the text(s).

(b) *Analysis*
    The response explains accurately and in detail ways in which relevant aspects of structure/style/language contribute to meaning/effect/impact.

(c) *Evaluation*
    The response reveals clear engagement with the text(s) or aspects of the text(s) and stated or implied evaluation of effectiveness, substantiated with detailed and relevant evidence from the text(s).

(d) *Expression*
    Structure, style and language, including appropriate critical terminology, are deployed to communicate meaning clearly and develop a line of thought which is consistently relevant to purpose; spelling, grammar and punctuation are sufficiently accurate.

Critical Essay (Higher)—Supplementary Advice

This advice, which is supplementary to the Performance Criteria, is designed to assist with the placing of scripts within the full range of marks. However, the Performance Criteria as published give the primary definitions. The mark range for each Category is identified.

IV　　*8–11	III　　12–15	II　　16–19	I　　20–25
An essay which falls into this category may do so for a variety of reasons.	**Understanding** • Knowledge of the text(s), and a secure understanding of the central concerns will be used.	**Understanding** • Knowledge and understanding of the central concerns of the text(s) will be clearly demonstrated.	**Understanding** • Thorough knowledge and insight into the central concerns of the text(s) will be demonstrated at this level.
It could be • that it fails to achieve consistent technical accuracy. • or that any knowledge and understanding of the text(s) is not deployed as a response relevant to the task. • or that analysis and evaluation attempted are unconvincing. • or that the answer is simply too thin.	• to provide an answer relevant to the task. • Detailed reference to the text(s) to support the candidate's argument will be made.	• and deployed sensibly to form a sound developed answer which is relevant to the task. • Detailed reference to the text(s) will be used appropriately as evidence for the candidate's argument.	• and there will be a relevant, well-structured response to the demands of the task. • Extensive and skilful reference to the text(s) will be used appropriately as evidence for the argument.
	Analysis • There will be an accurate explanation of the contribution of literary/ linguistic techniques to the impact of the text.	**Analysis** • There will be analysis of literary/ linguistic techniques and how they affect the impact of the text(s).	**Analysis** • There will be a convincing evaluative analysis of the writer's literary and linguistic techniques.
	Evaluation • There will be a positive engagement with the text(s) which will state or imply an evaluation of its effectiveness.	**Evaluation** • There will be a positive engagement with the text(s) (which may be implicit) leading to a considered evaluative stance with respect to the text(s).	**Evaluation** • There will be an appreciative response allied to a committed stance with respect to the text(s) which may be implicit.
	Expression • Language will communicate the argument clearly, and there will be appropriate critical terminology deployed. Spelling, grammar and punctuation will be sufficiently accurate.	**Expression** • Language will be used confidently and the deployment of critical terminology will add to the strength of the candidate's argument.	**Expression** • The language used will be controlled and fluent, making accurate and appropriate use of critical terminology in pursuit of a skilful analysis.
		At this level there should be no doubt that the question has been answered out of a sound knowledge and understanding of the text(s).	An answer of this standard will give the impression that it is drawing skilfully on an extensive knowledge of the text(s) to focus on the demands of the question.

*Essays which are so deficient that they do not meet the criteria for Category IV should be awarded an appropriate mark from 0–7. Marks below 6 will be extremely rare – mostly for essays which are exceptionally short.